edexcel :::
...ing lives

Edexcel GCE History

The Changing Position of Women and the Suffrage Question c.1860–1930

Rosemary Rees

Series editors: Martin Collier   Rosemary Rees

Unit 2 Student Book

A PEARSON COMPANY

Heinemann is an imprint of Pearson Education Limited, a company incorporated in England and Wales, having its registered office at Edinburgh Gate, Harlow, Essex, CM20 2JE. Registered company number: 872828

www.heinemann.co.uk

Heinemann is a registered trademark of Pearson Education Limited

Text © Rosemary Rees 2008

First published 2008

14

10 9 8

British Library Cataloguing in Publication Data is available from the British Library on request.

ISBN 978 0 435308 11 7

Edited by Florence Production Ltd, Stoodleigh, Devon
Designed by Florence Production Ltd, Stoodleigh, Devon
Typeset by Florence Production Ltd, Stoodleigh, Devon
Produced by Florence Production Ltd, Stoodleigh, Devon
Original illustrations © Pearson Education Ltd 2008
Cover design by Siu Hang Wong
Picture research by Zooid Pictures
Printed in Malaysia, CTP-PJB

Acknowledgements
The author and publisher would like to thank the following individuals and organisations for permission to reproduce photographs:

© Bridgeman Art Library p.7; © British Library Newspapers p.21, p.123; © Central Press / Getty Images p.111; © Hulton-Deutsch Collection / Corbis UK Ltd. p.78, p.85; ©Imperial War Museum p.107; © Mansell / Time Life Pictures / Getty Images p.110; © Mary Evans Picture Library p.9, p.23; © Mary Evans Picture Library / Alamy p.105; © Museum of London Picture Library p.87; © Museum of London / HIP / TopFoto p.68, p.69, p.90, p.101, p.111; © The National Archives / HIP / TopFoto p.73; © PA Photos p.71; © The Print Collector / Alamy p.31; © Punch Limited/TopFoto p.82, p.116; © Tate p.1; © TopFoto p.13, p.89; © Topham Picturepoint / PA Photos p.91; © The Women's Library - London Metropolitan University p.26, p.100.

Every effort has been made to contact copyright holders of material reproduced in this book. Any omissions will be rectified in subsequent printings if notice is given to the publishers.

Websites
The websites used in this book were correct and up-to-date at the time of publication. It is essential for tutors to preview each website before using it in class so as to ensure that the URL is still accurate, relevant and appropriate. We suggest that tutors bookmark useful websites and consider enabling students to access them through the school/college intranet.

Dedication
This book is dedicated, with love, to my granddaughters Bethan and Amelia, in the certainty that they will never remain silent when women's rights are threatened or ignored.

Contents

Introduction

The photograph opposite was taken in a London garden in the 1930s.

It shows an elderly grandmother, Martha, her middle-aged daughter Agnes and Elsie, her grown-up granddaughter. Just three women enjoying spending time together, with someone on hand to take a snapshot for the family photograph album. It is an ordinary snapshot of an ordinary family, and at first sight there doesn't seem to be anything particularly special about it.

What makes this ordinary family extraordinary is that all three of them lived through a time of profound and sometimes tumultuous change in the position of women in British society.

Behind every picture lies a story

What sort of lives had these women led?

Martha Carpenter (1849–1947):

- born into a family of farm labourers in Hertfordshire;
- never went to school but taught herself to read and write from her children's books;
- worked as a lady's maid in London until she married;
- married George Crane, a brewer's drayman, on Christmas Day 1876;
- after marriage worked at home, taking in sewing;
- three daughters (Alice, Agnes and Rose) and one son (Henry).

Agnes Crane (1883–1967):

- third child of Martha and George;
- attended a Board school 1888–93;
- apprenticed in a large sewing room making clothes for London shops;
- married Albert Woolfe, a post office sorter, in 1904 and had to stop full-time work;
- did occasional, part-time sewing at home when necessary;
- two daughters (Elsie and Constance) and one son (Leonard).

Elsie Woolfe (1908–1997):

- second child and first daughter of Agnes and Albert;
- won a scholarship to a London high school and then went to a secretarial college;
- worked as a secretary and personal assistant;
- married Alfred Gardner, a City of London policeman, in September 1934;
- continued working after marriage until she retired, aged sixty;
- no children.

Key national dates affecting Martha, Agnes and Elsie:

1867	Reform Act gave the vote to working-class men in towns
1870	Education Act sets up enough schools (called Board schools) for every child to have access to an elementary education
1880	Elementary education made compulsory
1882	Invention of the typewriter sees growth in shorthand and typewriting jobs for women
1884	Reform Act gave the vote to two men in every three
1891	Elementary education made free and compulsory up to the age of twelve
1891	Census records that women make up 59 per cent of the workforce in the clothing trade
1893	School leaving age fixed at eleven
1899	School leaving age raised to twelve
1902	Scholarships established to enable clever children from poor homes to progress to secondary schools
1906	Enquiry into women's work by Edward Cadbury reveals that most women believe it is right that they should earn less than men doing the same job
1910	Fewer than 10 per cent of married women in paid employment
1918	Women over the age of thirty given the vote
1928	Universal suffrage for men and women aged twenty-one and over on equal terms

Tasks

1 For each woman, Martha first, then Agnes and then Elsie, work out:

  i   her educational opportunities

  ii her workplace opportunities

  iii her right to vote in national elections and whether these differed from those of the men they married.

2 Find an image of at least one woman, dated between 1860 and 1935. This can be a family photograph, an historical portrait or an image from the Internet. The woman can be rich or poor or somewhere in between. Work out:

  i   what educational opportunities were likely to have been open to her

  ii what work opportunities were likely to have been open to her

  iii when, or whether, she was able to vote in general elections.

We don't know whether or not Martha, Agnes or Elsie were involved in writing letters and pamphlets campaigning for women's rights. We don't know whether they marched with the suffragists or chained themselves to railings with the suffragettes. But we do know that the actions of people who did had a profound effect on millions of ordinary British women like Martha, Agnes and Elsie. It is about these people you will read in this book, and about the ways in which they battled, not always successfully, to change the role and position of all women in British society.

UNIT

1 Mid-century women: philosophy and reality

What is this unit about?

This unit focuses on the ideas underpinning the attitudes of many Victorians to the role and significance of women in their society. In it you will:

- find out about the concept of the 'angel in the house' and how this related to the idea that men and women occupied 'separate spheres';
- test the 'angel in the house' and 'separate spheres' philosophies by relating them to reality.

Key questions

- What was the attitude of mid-Victorian people to women?
- To what extent was this attitude reflected in reality?

Woman's mission?

Look at this picture. It's a Victorian **narrative painting**. So what is the story here?

Source A

1.1 *Woman's Mission: Companion of Manhood* by George Elgar Hicks

SKILLS BUILDER

Quickly, before you read any further, what is the story behind this painting? What has been happening before this snapshot in time? Jot it down. Compare what you think with others in your group.

In 1863 an artist, George Elgar Hicks, painted a series of three paintings called 'Woman's Mission'. The first picture, called *The Guide of Childhood* shows a mother caring for and supporting her children; the third picture *The Comfort of Old Age,* shows an old man being looked after by his faithful daughter. This picture, the middle one in the series, is called *Companion of Manhood*. It's easy, just by reading the titles of the three paintings, to guess at the message the artist was attempting to convey: that woman's mission was to support the man and care for his home and children.

But look more closely to check out your guess.

- The husband has clearly had a shock. It probably concerns the death of someone close to him because in his hand is a letter with black edges and an envelope with black edges lies on the floor. This was the Victorian way of announcing a death.

- The couple are not sharing their grief, neither is the husband breaking the sad news gently to his wife. Instead, the wife is shown as being solely concerned with comforting her distressed husband. Just look at the expression on her face.

- The elaborate interior of the room and the elegant clothes of the couple indicate that the husband is successful at his work, whatever that is. He is the breadwinner, and can afford a good standard of living for his family.

- The clean and well ordered room, the delicate china on the table, the meal (even though it has been interrupted by bad news) all indicate that the woman is a good housekeeper, as a good wife should be.

So far, the original guess seems to have been correct: woman's mission is to support her husband and care for his needs, his house and his family. This, however, could be the view of just one artist. The popularity of the painting, though, should lead us to believe otherwise.

What was the 'angel in the house'?

The concept of the '**angel in the house**' was central to Victorian beliefs about the proper ordering of society. Woman's role was essentially domestic, creating a comfortable and loving home where her husband and children would be supported and protected from the evils of the world outside. This is neatly and succinctly described by the poet Tennyson in Source B.

Definition

'Angel in the house'

In 1854 Coventry Patmore wrote a poem called 'The Angel in the House'. In the poem, he made it clear that a wife's function was to please her husband, not just in his bed but by making his home a peaceful haven from the troubles and strains of the world, and by bringing up his children properly. She was, in fact, the 'angel in the house', bringing peace, love and contentment to all and never considering her own wants and needs.

Source B

... but this is fix'd
As are the roots of earth and base of all.
Man for the field and woman for the hearth;
Man for the sword and for the needle she:
Man with the head and woman with the heart:
All else confusion ...
From Alfred, Lord Tennyson *The Princess* published in 1847

Indeed, destroying this balance, it was argued time and time again by those who opposed **female emancipation**, would lead to the complete disruption of society.

Who was the first 'angel'?

The very first 'angel in the house' was Emily, the wife of Coventry Patmore. Believing she was the perfect wife, he wrote a poem about her called 'The Angel in the House'. The extract in Source C from this complicated, long and very sentimental poem gives some idea of what Coventry Patmore believed was the ideal husband–wife relationship.

Source C

Man must be pleased; but him to please is woman's pleasure.

And if he once, by shame oppressed
A comfortable word confers,
She leans and weeps against his breast,
And seems to think the sin was hers ...

She loves with love that cannot tire;
And when, ah woe, she loves alone,
Through passionate duty love springs higher,
As grass grows taller round a stone.
From Coventry Patmore *The Angel in the House* published in 1854

The implication here is that woman's role is **altruistic**: she exists to give pleasure and it is in giving pleasure to others she herself is pleased, is happy. She must give pleasure to her husband not just in his bed, but in everything she does in his home in creating peace and order for him and for his children.

And the husband? If he speaks sharply to his wife, or ill-treats her in any way, then she must blame herself even if he regrets what has been said or done. The meaning of the last verse is that even though husbands do stop loving wives, this is no reason for a wife to stop loving her husband.

Although the poem didn't attract much attention when it was first published in 1854, it became increasingly popular throughout the nineteenth century as women's demands for greater equality with men became increasingly vocal and most men and some women, desperately tried to maintain the status quo.

Definition

Female emancipation

To emancipate a person or a specific group of people (such as slaves) literally means to release them from control or restraint. In this context, therefore, female emancipation means to release women from legislative and social controls that prevented them from participating in society on the same terms as men.

Definition

Altruistic

When a person acts in the interest of others, rather than themselves.

Question

What do you think a woman's response would be to this? Remember to think in Victorian terms, not those of the twenty-first century. Would you feel secure, frustrated or used? Or something different?

This theme of the innate goodness and gentleness of women as wives, was picked up by the essayist John Ruskin.

Question

No woman could be all of these things. Why did Ruskin, then, suggest that this is what a woman should be? How does this relate to Coventry Patmore's view of woman's role?

Source D

She must be enduringly, incorruptibly good; instinctively, infallibly wise – wise, not for self development, but for self renunciation; wise, not that she may set herself above her husband, but that she may never fall from his side; wise, not with the narrowness of insolent and loveless pride, but with the passionate gentleness of an infinitely variable, because infinitely applicable, modesty of service.

From John Ruskin *Sesame and Lilies* published in 1865

The 'angel in the house' here has to maintain the ideal of service to her husband and develop a wisdom that will enable her to support him throughout his life.

It is perhaps worth noting that John Ruskin himself had an unhappy first marriage. His marriage to Effie Gray in 1848 was **annulled** after six years because of his impotency. It is said that he fainted when he saw her naked body and realised she had pubic hair. In a letter to his lawyer explaining why he didn't consummate his marriage on his wedding night, Ruskin explained that her body 'did not excite passion'.

Question

Given Ruskin's personal life, how are we to trust what he says about women?

However, what Ruskin said about womankind was generally believed. Women were gentle, weak and tender. They had to be protected from the cut and thrust of the working world outside the home. The home was a sacred place and women, the guardians of this sacred place, were to be cherished and idealised.

How were women to create a 'proper' home?

Many women were far from being the weak, passive creatures that the 'angel in the house' concept seems to convey. Mrs Beeton very briskly provided a practical and positive approach to the problem of managing a household.

Definition

Annulment

When a marriage is annulled it is as if, legally, it never happened. An annulment is usually granted when sexual intercourse has not occurred. An annulment is different from a divorce, when sexual intercourse has happened and there are often children as a result.

Source E

As with the commander of an army, or the leader of any enterprise, so it is with the mistress of a house. Having risen early, and given due attention to the bath and made a careful toilet, it will be well at once to see that the children have received their proper ablutions, and are in every way clean and comfortable. After breakfast is over, it will be well for the mistress to make a round of the kitchen and other offices, to see that all are in order, and that the morning's work has been properly performed by the various domestics. The orders for the day should then be given. After luncheon, visits may be made and received. The next great event of the day in most establishments is 'The Dinner'.

From Isabella Beeton *Beeton's Book of Household Management* published in 1861

Even those middle-class women whose husbands could not afford the sort of establishment Mrs Beeton is writing about, were able to perform their duties as 'angels in the house'. Source F is part of the obituary of Frances Goodby, the late wife of the Reverend J. Goodby of Ashby-de-la-Zouch in Leicestershire.

Source F

Her ardent and unceasing flow of spirits, extreme activity and diligence, her punctuality, uprightness and remarkable frugality, combined with a firm reliance on God, carried her through the severest times of pressure, both with credit and respectability.

From *The General Baptist Repository and Missionary Observer*, published in 1840

Question

Have a guess. Given what you know about Victorian society so far, what might Frances Goodby have felt about her lot in life?

It is not known what Mrs Goodby herself thought about her lot in life.

Although many women accepted their role willingly and, indeed, revelled in it, there were some who did not. Florence Nightingale wrote an unpublished autobiographical novel in 1854 about the intolerable nature of such a life. Many would have agreed with her.

Source G

Women are never supposed to have any occupation of importance except 'suckling their fools'; and women themselves have accepted this, have written books to support it, and have trained themselves so as to consider whatever they do as not of such value to the world as others, but that they can throw it up at the first claim on their time. They have accustomed themselves to consider intellectual occupation as a merely selfish amusement, which it is their duty to give up for every trifler more selfish than themselves.

Women never have an half-hour in all their lives (except before and after anybody is up in the house) that they can call their own, without fear of offending or hurting someone. Why do women sit up late, or, more rarely, get up so early? Not because the day is not long enough, but because they have no time in the day for themselves.

The family? It is too narrow a field for the development of an immortal spirit, be that spirit male or female. The family uses people, not for what they are, not for what they are intended to be, but for what it wants for its own uses. It thinks of them not as what God has made them, but as the something which it has arranged that they shall be. This system dooms some minds to incurable infancy, others to silent misery.

From Florence Nightingale *Cassandra* written in 1854

Question

Florence's friends persuaded her not to allow her book to be published. Why do you think this was?

Denied the opportunity to contribute in the workplace, middle-class women were pushed more and more into an almost ornamental role. The amount of leisure hours they had at their disposal, their jewellery, their fashionable clothes and the luxury of their homes told of their husbands' success. It was these middle-class, intelligent, under-used, frustrated and bored women that formed a substantial part of the articulate drive for female emancipation.

How did unmarried women fit the 'angel in the house' image?

The quick answer to this question is that they didn't. A longer answer focuses on a major problem in Victorian England, that of surplus women. The 1851 census revealed that 29 per cent (2,765,000) of all women over the age of twenty were unmarried; by 1871 this figure had risen to 3,288,000. In 1871 two-thirds of all women aged between twenty and twenty-four were single, and 30 per cent of those aged twenty-four to thirty. For every three women over twenty who were wives, there were two who were widowed or who had never married. The distress caused by the 'surplus women' problem was keenly felt among the middle classes, where the prohibitions on women working were greatest and the gender gap the widest.

The reasons for this are not hard to find.

- Male mortality in childhood was higher than female and so more girls than boys survived into adulthood.
- Many men of marriageable age, attracted by good livings to be made in the empire, had emigrated. For example, in 1861, 124,000 men emigrated as against 41,000 women.
- The rising cost of living meant that the middle-class male tended to postpone marriage until he could afford to run a suburban villa and keep a wife and children in the manner in which he thought they should be kept.

Whatever the reason, or combination of reasons, middle-class single women were a problem. They were a problem because they were regarded as social failures. Lacking a husband to provide for them, they were usually forced to live in lonely lodgings on small **annuities** provided for them by a brother or father, and devote themselves to good works. Unsurprisingly, the impetus for change came from this group, too.

Separate spheres: what were they?

The concepts of the 'angel in the house' and '**separate spheres**' were in reality two sides of the same coin. It was only a short step from seeing husband and wife as performing different roles in their domestic situation to believing that men and women must perform different, separate roles in society at large.

In a very real sense, these attitudes were a product of the industrial revolution. By physically separating the home and the workplace, women

Definition

Annuities

A yearly allowance: a sum of money paid to an individual every year.

Separate spheres

This is the idea that men and women occupy separate and different spheres in society. Men work outside the home, in factories, offices and in government. Women work inside the home, making sure it is a fitting refuge for men from the stresses and strains of everyday life.

Question

How do you think single women would have reacted to finding that they were considered to be 'surplus women'?

lost touch with the production process. As their husbands' work moved to factories and commercial centres, women began to focus on the home, devoting themselves to childcare and matters domestic. The idea grew that men should have a wage sufficient to keep a family and that married women contributed economically to the family unit and to the country by running their homes.

Did women work in Victorian Britain?

The prohibition on middle-class women working was very strong. If you worked, you were not a lady. If you worked, you could certainly not fulfil your 'angel in the house' role.

It was just about possible for middle-class women to work as dressmakers, milliners or governesses, but to take on such occupations did signal to the interested world that you, and probably your family, had fallen on hard times.

The role of the governess is a particularly poignant one. They appear frequently in novels of the period and the way they are portrayed does seem to mirror reality more or less accurately. They live with well-off families in a sort of limbo, neither guest, nor relative, nor servant. Their relationship with the parents and with the children themselves is frequently ambiguous. They are usually widows, abandoned wives or unmarried women with some education, and therefore probably middle-class themselves, but who are, for whatever reason, in straightened circumstances.

Source H

A lady, to be such, must be a mere lady and nothing else. She must not work for profit, or engage in any occupation that money can command, lest she invade the rights of the working classes, who live by their labour.

From the diary of Margaretta Greg written in 1853

Source I

1.2 *The Governess*, painted by Richard Redgrave in 1844

SKILLS BUILDER

1 What 'message' is the artist trying to get across to his audience? There is a pile of books to be marked on the table; the governess is holding a black-edged letter; there is a solitary meal on the table; the music on the piano is 'Home, Sweet Home'.

2 Look at the girl seated on the right of the painting. What is she thinking? Have an inspired guess – but keep it in context.

Definition

Domestic service

This phrase usually relates to the work women do in rich and well-to-do homes. They work as cooks and kitchen maids, as ladies' maids and nursery maids, as housemaids and housekeepers. Men also enter domestic service, but as butlers, valets and boot-boys.

The last line in the extract from Margaretta Greg's diary (Source H) gives a strong lead as to the attitude of middle-class women to working-class women. They worked because they had to. Indeed, it would have been impossible for middle-class women to fulfil their function as angels in the house without having other women work for them. In 1851, 25.7 per cent of the total female population were working; ten years later this had risen to 26.3 per cent. The vast majority of these women were in **domestic service**, followed by working in textiles, clothing and agriculture.

Enquiries into working conditions for women revealed horrific conditions in sweatshops, factories and mines. Indeed, the 1842 Mines Act specifically forbade women to work underground – a move fiercely resisted by some women underground workers, forced to become 'pit brow girls'. There was a widespread belief that factory work degraded women.

Source J

Factory women meet together to drink, sing and smoke; they use, it is stated, the lowest, most brutal and most disgusting language imaginable.

From a speech made by Lord Shaftesbury in parliament in 1846. He was speaking in favour of the Ten Hours' Bill, which became law in 1847.

Ten years later, the Trades Union Congress supported restrictions on women's work, as illustrated in Source K.

Source K

It was their duty as men and husbands to use their utmost efforts to bring about a condition of things where their wives should be in their proper sphere at home, seeing after their house and family, instead of being dragged into the competition for livelihood against the great and strong men of the world.

From a speech made by Henry Broadhurst, President of the TUC, to the TUC in 1877

SKILLS BUILDER

How far do Sources J and K relate to the 'angel in the house' concept?

Source L

1.3 Colliery lasses of Wigan, 1900

Unit summary

What have you learned in this unit?

The 'angel in the house' and the 'separate spheres' concepts dominated Victorian attitudes to middle- and upper-class women, restricting their activities to the domestic sphere. Dependent on working-class women to support this concept, their attitude to them was at best ambivalent and at worst condemnatory.

These basic attitudes to women were to be challenged by attacking inequalities wherever and whenever they appeared: in the home, in educational opportunities, in the workplace and the **suffrage**.

What skills have you used in this unit?

You have evaluated a range of different sorts of source material, cross-referencing between them and drawing inferences from them. You have then used the understanding you have gained to test a hypothesis.

Definition

Suffrage

The right to vote.

SKILLS BUILDER

1 Work in threes. Each of you must choose one woman:

   (i)   Martha (see Introduction page v)

   (ii)   The governess (Source I page 7)

   (iii) A colliery lass (Source L page 9).

Work out how the twin concepts of 'separate spheres' and 'angel in the house' could relate to her.

How would she explain it?

Have a discussion in role.

2 Set up a formal debate on the motion 'This house believes that the concepts of "separate spheres" and the "angel in the house" were devices to control women.' Remember that someone will have to propose the motion and someone oppose it (and explain why) before everyone else can join in the discussion. There will have to be a vote at the end.

3 Why could any challenge to the concepts of 'separate spheres' and 'angel in the house' be seen as a challenge to the structure of society as a whole? Explain your answer using the sources and information in this unit.

Exam tips

This is the sort of question you will find appearing on the examination papers as an (a) question.

Study Sources A, B and D.

How far do Sources B and D support the attitude to women shown in Source A?

- **Don't** bring in a lot of your own knowledge. All (a) questions focus on the analysis, cross-referencing and evaluation of source material. Your own knowledge won't be credited by the examiner, and you will waste valuable time writing it out.

- **Do** remember that the only own knowledge you should introduce will be to put the sources into context. This means, for example, that you might explain that Source A is a narrative painting, or that John Ruskin had an unhappy marriage.

- **Don't** describe (or even re-write) the sources: the examiner will have a copy of the exam paper!

- **Do** draw inferences from the sources concerning what they show about attitudes to women, and cross-reference the inferences for similarity and difference.

- **Do** reach a supported judgement about 'how far' Sources B and D support Source A by carefully weighing the similarities and differences.

SKILLS BUILDER

Now try this question. Remember that this one is not asking about support, but about challenge. The approach, however, should be the same and you should use the exam tips in the same way.

4 Study Sources C, E and G.

To what extent does Source G challenge the 'angel in the house' described in Sources C and E?

RESEARCH TASK

Mary Wollstonecraft

In 1792, Mary Wollstonecraft wrote a book called *A Vindication of the Rights of Women*.

- Who was Mary Wollstonecraft?

- What were the main points she made in her book?

- What impact did her book have at the time?

- Are you surprised that she wrote when she did? (Hint: think about the key dates of 1776 and 1789.)

- To what extent do you think it strange that women were still arguing about and fighting for their rights sixty years later?

2 How did women's personal lives change 1860–1901?

What is this unit about?

This unit focuses on the ways in which legislation during this period brought about changes in women's personal lives, and on the campaigns that led to successful legislation being passed by parliament. In it you will:

- find out about the relevant legislation;
- work with source material to evaluate the impact of the campaigns on decision makers in parliament and analyse the effectiveness of the legislation.

Key questions

- To what extent did women gain control over their personal lives during this period?
- How far did women gain experience of campaigning on personal and sexual issues at this time?

Timeline

1839	Custody of Children Act
1857	Matrimonial Causes Act
1864	First Contagious Diseases Act
1866	Second Contagious Diseases Act
1869	Third Contagious Diseases Act Josephine Butler forms the Ladies National Association
1870	First Married Woman's Property Act
1873	Second Custody of Infants Act
1882	Second Married Woman's Property Act
1883	Contagious Diseases Act suspended
1884	Women acquire independent legal status
1885	Age of consent raised from thirteen to sixteen
1886	Married Women (Maintenance in Case of Desertion) Act Guardianship of Infants Act Repeal of Contagious Diseases Act
1891	The Jackson case: a man cannot compel his wife to live with him

Source A

2.1 *Past and Present* painted by Augustus Egg in 1858

SKILLS BUILDER

Unit 1 began with a narrative painting and this unit is doing the same. This time, however, the meaning of the painting isn't going to be unpacked for you. You're going to do it! Think about:

- the distressed state of the wife;
- the letter the husband is holding;
- the picture the husband is grinding under foot;
- the apple;
- the house of cards built by the children.

1 What 'story' is the painting telling?

2 What do you think the apple and the house of cards represent?

To what extent were there double standards in sexual morality in Victorian times?

Men and women, husbands and wives, were expected to live by different standards when it came to personal relationships. This all goes back to the 'angel in the house' and 'separate spheres' philosophies. Part of a wife's role in being an 'angel in the house' was to provide an antidote for her husband to the harsh world of work and its corrupting influences that he inhabited. A wife, with her delicate female sensitivities, was expected to have a positive influence on her husband, leading him to a higher moral plane. You can guess where this argument is going! It therefore followed that if a man was unfaithful to his wife, he was simply allowing his animal feelings to get the better of him. An unfaithful wife, on the other hand, was not only betraying her husband but also her children, her home and her wider family because she should have been operating on a higher moral plane and helping her whole family, and especially her husband, achieve this moral high ground, too. A husband's adultery was regarded as an understandable and probably pardonable lapse because he was, after all, at the mercy of his natural instincts. A wife's adultery, on the other hand, was a serious and unpardonable offence because she was betraying hers.

Definition

Condone

Accept or allow bad actions or behaviour to continue.

Question

Two reasons have been advanced here for regarding a wife's adultery as more serious than that of a husband. What are they? Which do you find the more convincing? Why?

Definition

Legal identity

To be recognised by the law. In the case of married women at this time, they were not recognised as being legally separate people from their husbands.

Source B

A wife might without any loss of status and possibly with reference to the interests of her children, or even of her husband, **condone** an act of adultery on the part of her husband. But a husband could not condone a similar act on the part of a wife. No one would venture to suggest that a husband could possibly do so and for this reason, among other reasons, that the adultery of the wife might be the means of palming spurious offspring upon the husband while the adultery of the husband could have no such effect with regard to the wife.

From a speech in the House of Lords made by Lord Chancellor Cranworth in 1857, quoted in *Hansard*, where he gives an additional, practical reason for condemning a wife's adultery

Behind this idea is fear and insecurity as well as notions of property and inheritance. A husband with an adulterous wife could never, in the days before DNA testing, be certain that 'his' children were biologically his. After his death, the husband's property might be inherited by children who were not his, in the sense they were not of his blood, but whom he had been led to believe were children of the marriage. Thus unknowingly property could pass out of the family, away from the bloodline. The security of his family, his biological family, would be threatened. To Victorians, this was very important.

How legally secure were married women?

In the mid-nineteenth century, married women had virtually no status in law, and neither did the law offer them much protection. A married woman had no separate **legal identity** from her husband and consequently could not own property in her own right. Thus once a woman married, all the property she owned before her marriage and brought with her to the marriage and all her earnings once she was married became the property of her husband. He could do with them as he wished. The children of the marriage were his and his wife had no legal rights over them. A husband had complete care and control of his children and could refuse his wife access to them.

Source C

The disabilities a woman lies under are for the most part intended for her protection and benefit, so great a favourite is the female sex in the laws of England.

> From William Blackstone *Commentaries on the Laws of England* first published in 1765 and in continuous print throughout the nineteenth century. Blackstone was a judge and an expert on family law

Technically, Blackstone was correct. If a woman, for example, committed a crime in the presence of her husband (except murder and treason) the law said that she must have been coerced and so was guiltless. Women, because they could own nothing, were not held responsible for their own debts: the husband had to pay up.

There were ways round this. Wealthy families could take out complicated trusts that enabled their daughters to hold and use money in their own right but these were incredibly expensive to set up and administer. Few women knew about them and even fewer had families who took advantage of them.

Source D

The English family in the years following Waterloo [1815] differed in many ways from the family of today. The husband was in a very real sense the authoritarian head of the family, with very extensive powers over both person and property of his wife and children. On marriage, husband and wife became for many purposes one person in law. On marriage all the wife's personal chattels [goods] became the absolute property of the husband, while the husband could dispose of the wife's property during his life and enjoyed for his own benefit her estate during her life, the married woman, both physically and economically, was very much in the position of chattel of her husband.

> From Professor Graveson *Family Law 1857–1957* published in 1966

SKILLS BUILDER

How likely is it that Professor Graveson would agree with the views of William Blackstone?

How did women begin to take control of their personal lives?

The position of married women, before late-Victorian legislation attempted to give married women more control over their lives, is highlighted by the case of Caroline Norton.

Case study: the case of Caroline Norton

Caroline Norton: more sinned against than sinning?

George Norton, the Tory MP for Guildford, fell in love with Caroline Sheridan when she was just sixteen years old. Although she didn't return his feelings, she agreed to marry him in order to help her widowed mother's desperate financial situation. The couple married in 1827 when Caroline was nineteen. They had three sons: Fletcher (1829), Brinsley (1831) and William (1833). But all was not as it seemed. The marriage was a disaster. Caroline found her husband boring and lazy, and she did not attempt to hide her feelings. George responded by beating her and on several occasions the servants had to restrain him in order to prevent him inflicting serious physical damage. George lost his seat in parliament in the 1830 election and asked Caroline to use her influence with Whig politicians to get him a job. Caroline did as he asked, using her contact with Lord Melbourne, the Home Secretary, and George became a magistrate in the Lambeth Division of the Metropolitan Police Courts, with a generous salary. Lord Melbourne, a widower and a renowned womaniser, and Caroline became close friends. Rumours began to circulate. George heard these rumours but did nothing, hoping that Caroline's friendship with Lord Melbourne would benefit him. George continued to beat Caroline from time to time and on two occasions she left him, but returned because she didn't want to lose her children. George then complained that Melbourne (who became Prime Minister in March 1835) wasn't doing enough to help him and began to leak stories to the Tory press about the relationship between Caroline and Melbourne. George, desperate for money and hoping Melbourne would settle out of court, sued Melbourne in June 1836 for 'alienating his wife's affections' and lost. George then turned on Caroline. He refused her entry to their home and sent their three sons to Scotland, so that all ties with her would be broken. George only permitted the children to see their mother in September 1842 when William, the youngest boy, died as the result of an accident. But this was no rapprochement, although George allowed their two remaining sons to live with Caroline. George discovered that, when Melbourne died in 1848, he left a small legacy to Caroline; so did her mother, who died in 1851. When Caroline refused to hand over the money (which legally was his) George refused to pay the money agreed between them that he would contribute for the upkeep of their remaining two sons. He also steadfastly refused to give Caroline the divorce she so badly wanted that would enable her to marry Sir William Stirling-Maxwell, the man with whom she had had a relationship for over twenty-five years. Caroline could not divorce him for adultery because, although George had had adulterous affairs, she had forgiven him and taken him back into their marriage afterwards. The situation was resolved in 1877 when George died. Caroline, then aged sixty-nine, finally married Sir William, but died three months later.

Question

Tease out the part played by George in this sad little story. How would he defend his actions? What might he have said to Caroline towards the end of her life to justify the way in which he treated her?

Now read these sources that give you Caroline's point of view:

Source E

We had been married about two months, when, one evening we were discussing some opinion Mr Norton had expressed. I said that 'I thought I had never heard so silly or ridiculous a conclusion.' This remark was punished by a sudden and violent kick; the blow reached my side; it caused great pain for several days.

Four or five months afterwards, when we were settled in London, we had returned home from a ball. Unexpectedly, Mr Norton indulged in bitter and coarse remarks respecting a young relative of mine, who, though married, continued to dance – a practice, Mr Norton said, no husband ought to permit. I defended the lady spoken of when he suddenly sprang from the bed, seized me by the nape of the neck, and dashed me down on the floor. The sound of my fall woke my sister and brother-in-law, who slept in a room below, and they ran up to the door. Mr Norton locked it, and stood over me, declaring no one should enter. I could not speak – I only moaned. My brother-in-law burst the door open and carried me downstairs. I had a swelling on my head for many days afterwards.

From Caroline Norton's account of the early
years of her marriage, written in 1854

Source F

After the adultery trial was over, I learnt the law as to my children – that the right was with the father; that neither my innocence nor his guilt could alter it; that not even his giving them into the hands of a mistress, would give me any claim to their custody. The eldest was but six years old, the second four, the youngest two and a half, when we were parted. I wrote, therefore, and petitioned the father and husband in whose power I was, for leave to see them – for leave to keep them, till they were a little older. Mr Norton's answer was, that I should not have them; that if I wanted to see them, I might have an interview with them at the chambers of his attorney. What I suffered on my children's account, none will ever know or measure. Mr Norton held my children as hostages; he felt that while he had them, he still had power over me that nothing could control.

From Caroline Norton *English Laws for Women in
the Nineteenth Century* published in 1854

SKILLS BUILDER

1 Now think about the situation from Caroline's point of view. What could she have done differently? What should she have done according to the standards of the time? Discuss this with a partner.

2 Think about both George and Caroline. What conclusion can you reach: was Caroline Norton more sinned against than sinning? Again, discuss this with a partner and reach a conclusion.

3 Caroline Norton was no weak-willed woman. The attribution to Source F should give you a clue as to how she reacted to her situation. What is the clue?

How did Caroline Norton work to try to change married women's personal lives?

1 Regarding children

Caroline Norton was an accomplished poet and writer of fiction. However, it was her political writing that had the most impact.

- After George Norton had lost his court case against Lord Melbourne and Caroline realised she had 'lost' her children, she wrote a pamphlet *The Natural Claim of a Mother to the Custody of her Children as Affected by the Common Law Rights of the Father.* Not exactly a snappy title – but she needed to make it clear what she was writing about so as to catch the attention of MPs and lawyers, as well as articulate women, who could perhaps begin to make moves towards changing the law. In the pamphlet she set about explaining the unfairness of a system that could find a woman innocent of adultery and still allow her husband to prevent her from seeing their children. Under the current law, she argued, a father had absolute rights, no matter what his behaviour, and a mother no rights at all.

- In 1838, Caroline began a campaign to get the law changed. She persuaded Sir Thomas Talfourd, the MP for Reading, to support her cause. He introduced a bill into parliament that would allow mothers, against whom adultery had not been proved, to have custody of their children if they were under seven years old, with rights of access to older children. The bill was passed by the House of Commons but rejected by the House of Lords.

- Undaunted, Caroline wrote another pamphlet: *A Plain Letter to the Lord Chancellor on the Law of Custody of Infants.* A copy of the pamphlet was sent to every MP.

- In 1839, Talfourd tried again. This time he succeeded. His bill was passed in both Houses of Parliament and passed in to law.

What did the Custody of Children Act of 1839 say?

The Act gave to mothers the right of custody of their children under seven, but only if the **Lord Chancellor** agreed to it, and only if the mother was of good character.

In 1886, parliament passed the Guardianship of Infants Act. This gave women even more of a chance to gain custody of their children. The Act stated that, when determining which parent should have custody, the welfare of the child (or children) should be taken into account.

2 Regarding marriage

- When Caroline refused to hand over her legacies to her husband and he countered by refusing to support their children, she took to campaigning again.

- Part of Caroline's campaigning involved pamphlet writing. The two most powerful ones were *English Laws for Women in the Nineteenth*

Question

To what extent do you think this Act was a significant breakthrough for women?

Definition

Lord Chancellor

Person responsible for government policy on the legal system, head of the judiciary and presides over the House of Lords.

Century (1854) and *A Letter to the Queen on Lord Cranworth's Marriage and Divorce Bill* (1855).

- In 1857, partly as a result of Caroline's efforts, parliament passed the Divorce and Matrimonial Causes Act.

What did the Divorce and Matrimonial Causes Act of 1857 say?

The Act allowed for divorce to happen through the law courts instead of, as before, by a private Act of Parliament, which was both slow and very expensive. In order for a husband to divorce his wife, he had to prove her adultery. But if a wife wanted to divorce her husband, she had to prove not only adultery, but either bigamy, rape, sodomy, bestiality, cruelty or long-term desertion as well.

Caroline's experiences, about which she made no secret during her campaigning, influenced the insertion of other clauses in the Act:

- A wife deserted by her husband could keep her own income.
- The courts were able to order payment of maintenance to a wife.
- A wife was able to inherit and bequeath property the same as a single woman.
- A wife separated from her husband could sue, and be sued, in a civil court.

Caroline Norton did not act alone in her campaigns. She had a great deal of support from women who had been similarly affected as well as those who were beginning to feel that the 'angel in the house' and 'separate spheres' philosophies should be challenged. Perhaps most importantly of all, she had understood the necessity of gaining the support of MPs and so of impacting on the Houses of Parliament. Changing attitudes in the country at large was vitally important, but in the end it was the Houses of Parliament that had to be convinced.

What was the significance of the Jackson case of 1891?

In 1884 a Matrimonial Causes Act denied a husband the right to lock up his wife if she refused to have sex with him. This went some way to lessen wife-battering and marital rape by beginning to indicate that a husband's physical control over his wife was not absolute. In 1891 it was the appeal court judges' decision that reinforced this and provided **case law** on which other judges later relied.

A Mr Jackson returned from New Zealand, where he had been setting up a new business, to his home in Clitheroe, Lancashire. However, his wife refused to see him. More than a little annoyed, Mr Jackson worked out a cunning plan. Helped by a couple of friends, he grabbed his wife as she left church. They bundled her into his carriage and drove off to his house. There he locked her up. Luckily she had some good friends and they campaigned for her release. After a long legal struggle, the judges decided that Mr Jackson had no right to force his wife to live with him.

Questions

Why do you think different criteria applied to husbands and wives when they wanted to divorce? Think back to the 'angel in the house' and 'separate spheres' philosophies and discuss this in your group.

To what extent did the Divorce and Matrimonial Causes Act challenge the philosophy of the 'angel in the house'?

Definition

Case law

English law is based on case law. The way in which a particular judge interprets a law will be used by future judges when they have to make their decisions. All these decisions, taken together, form case law.

Question

How far did the Jackson case further challenge the 'angel in the house' philosophy?

How significant were the Married Women's Property Acts of 1870 and 1882?

The Married Women's Property Acts were significant in two main ways. They were significant because of the concessions they made to women's rights over what was, to all intents and purposes, their own property; and they were important because of the fact that women again organised themselves into a pretty effective pressure group.

- In 1854, **Barbara Leigh Smith** (later Barbara Bodichon, see page 22) began a campaign to change the laws on property. She began by writing articles, organising petitions and setting up an all-woman committee to progress matters.

- A petition containing 26,000 signatures was presented to parliament.

- The Law Amendment Society took up the cause and a bill was drawn up that proposed giving women certain property rights.

However, at the last moment the bill on women's property rights was withdrawn in order to allow the Divorce and Matrimonial Causes bill to go through parliament and become law. This was done because people were afraid that to present parliament with two bills concerned with changing the status of women would frighten MPs (remember all MPs were men at this time) into thinking that too much was being done too quickly and they would vote against both bills.

The 1867 Reform Act (see page 50) did not include women in the extended franchise, despite concerted efforts to persuade MPs to do so. Having lost on one front, it seemed sensible to try another, and to push once more for a re-think of women's property rights. This time, the women and their male supporters were successful. A first Married Women's Property Act was passed in 1870, followed by a second in 1882.

What did the Married Women's Property Acts say?

The first Married Women's Property Act allowed married women to keep up to £200 in earnings and personal property. The second Act gave married women control over all the property and money they brought with them into the marriage. It also allowed them to carry on with whatever trade or business they were working in before they were married, using their own property and money.

Why were the Acts passed?

The Married Women's Property Acts were passed for three main reasons:

- Cases like that of Caroline Norton had shown how unfair the law was in respect of married women, and general support for change had grown as a result.

- Women's groups (and their male supporters) were putting a considerable amount of pressure on parliament and they were learning various different strategies to make this pressure effective.

- Many Liberal MPs supported the Married Women's Property Acts because they believed that women only wanted the vote so that they could gain control over their own money and property. Give women this control, they argued, and pressure for the vote would fade away. They were wrong, but for the moment that didn't matter. What mattered was their support for the Married Women's Property Acts that carried them through both Houses of Parliament.

Questions

To what extent were the Married Women's Property Acts significant? Discuss this with a partner.

Married women were not given the same property rights as single women until 1935. Why do you think this was?

Source G

2.2 This cartoon was published on the front cover of the *Illustrated Police News* in April 1891

Source H

The paradox behind the double standard was once again all too visible. The critical point which emerged from the battles over divorce reform was that, for legislators, the dangerous sex was not female but male. If divorce was made easy and respectable, it was feared this would lead to serial polygamy because of the promiscuous sexual appetite of the human male. This was a view with which women were very much in agreement. It was a view that was to contradict the claim that the women's movement was about 'equality'. For while feminists went to war against the ill effects on women of the double standard, at the very same time they were to maintain that male sexual behaviour was dangerous and predatory, while female sexual behaviour was benign and moral. It was a paradox which was to allow their opponents to open up a deadly front against them – by agreeing that women were special, they had to be kept so.

From Melanie Phillips *The Ascent of Women* published in 2003

Biography

Barbara Leigh Smith 1827–1891

(Barbara Bodichon after she married Eugene Bodichon in 1857)

Barbara was born into a radical, free-thinking family:

- her grandfather worked closely with William Wilberforce in his campaign to abolish the slave trade;
- her great-grandfather sided with the American colonists in their fight for independence from the British in 1776;
- Florence Nightingale was a distant cousin;
- her parents never married – they couldn't see the point.

Barbara's father was a radical MP and, from a very young age Barbara was used to listening to, and joining in with, discussions on a range of controversial topics. Her father supported women's rights and Barbara was brought up in the same way as her four brothers. When the children became twenty-one, they were each given £300 a year and it was this annuity that enabled Barbara to throw herself into campaigning for women's rights. She:

- set up a progressive school in London that was co-educational, **non-denominational** and took children from a range of different backgrounds;
- worked with Caroline Norton on the campaign that resulted in the Divorce and Matrimonial Causes Act;
- wrote many pamphlets, the most influential of which were *A Brief Summary in Plain Language of the Most Important Laws Concerning Women* and *Women at Work* in 1857;
- founded in 1858, with Bessie Rayner Parkes, the feminist journal *The Englishwoman's Review*. This was important because it provided a forum for women campaigning for women doctors and for better opportunities in higher education;
- formed the first Women's Suffrage Committee in 1866, and toured the country holding meetings, converting many women to the cause of female suffrage;
- joined with Emily Davis in helping to raise funds for the first women's college (Girton) in Cambridge.

Definition

Non-denominational

Not connected to any particular religious group.

Why was the repeal of the Contagious Diseases Acts such an important cause?

The Contagious Diseases Acts were passed in an attempt by the Houses of Parliament to control female prostitution. It was the attitude of the male worlds of medicine and government to prostitution that exposed the double standards of sexual morality and provided tremendous momentum for women's rights.

To what extent was female prostitution a problem?

Source I

I should think that prostitution in England is considerably greater than in other countries. From mid-afternoon it is impossible for a respectable woman to walk from the top of Haymarket to Wellington Street off the Strand. The West End is thronged with prostitutes, openly soliciting.

> Howard Vincent, director of CID at Scotland Yard, gave evidence to a committee of peers in 1881. This is part of what he said.

Source J

All the houses, except one or two, are evidently inhabited by harlots [prostitutes]. Every hundred steps one jostles twenty harlots; some of them ask for a glass of gin; others say 'Sir, it is to pay my lodgings'. This is not **debauchery** which flaunts itself but destitution.

> From Hippolyte Taine *Notes on England* published in 1885. Here he is writing about Shadwell in the East End of London.

Source K

THE BEADLE OF THE BURLINGTON.—"SOMETIMES A SOVEREIGN, AND SOMETIMES LESS."

Definition

Debauchery

Sexual immorality.

SKILLS BUILDER

1 What are the differences and the similarities between the two accounts given in Sources I and J?

2 How far does Source H support Sources G and K?

2.3 Streetwalkers bribing the beadle to let them walk through Burlington Arcade, London.

It wasn't the nuisance of prostitution nor the suggestion of destitution, but something darker and more sinister that concerned the surgeon, William Acton.

Source L

Vice does not hide itself, it throngs our streets, intrudes into our parks and theatres and other places of resort, bringing to the foolish temptation, and knowledge of sin to the innocent; it invades the very sanctuary of home, destroying the happiness of marriages and blighting the hopes of parents. Nor is it indirectly only that our society is injured; prostitutes do not generally die in harness. They become, with tarnished bodies and polluted minds, wives and mothers; whilst among some classes of the people their moral sentiment is so depraved, that the woman who lives by the hire of her person is received on almost equal terms. It is clear, then, that though we call these women outcasts and **pariahs**, they have a powerful influence for evil on all ranks of the community. The moral injury inflicted on society by prostitution is incalculable; the physical injury is at least as great.

From William Acton *Prostitution*, published in 1857 and re-printed ten times in the following twelve years. He saw prostitution as a social problem and here he is explaining why.

Definition

Pariah

A social outcast.

Question

What is the 'moral injury' that William Acton believes prostitutes inflict on society? Think back to the 'angel in the house' philosophy and to the different standards of sexual behaviour expected of husbands and wives. Discuss this in your group and agree what the 'moral injury' was that Acton was so anxious about.

William Acton was also just as worried about what he referred to as 'physical injury'. By this he meant venereal disease. By the mid-nineteenth century, venereal disease was considered to be a serious threat to the nation as a whole. It was particularly severe among soldiers and, to a lesser extent, sailors. It was the armed forces that extensively used prostitutes because soldiers were discouraged from marrying – it was believed that married men would lack the will to go to war and risk their lives in battle. However, it wasn't just the armed forces that used prostitutes. In a society that expected its middle-class men, on the point of marriage, to be sexually experienced and its middle-class women to be virgins, prostitution flourished.

What did the Contagious Diseases Acts aim to do?

The driving force behind the Contagious Diseases Acts was the need to reduce the incidence of venereal disease. The authorities were convinced that preventative measures were needed. Venereal disease was spread through contact with infected prostitutes and, by the middle of the century, it was possible to diagnose and treat the condition. However, in 1859 compulsory medical examinations of soldiers was abandoned because of the hostility of the men to such intimate investigations. The spotlight therefore switched to the prostitutes themselves.

1 The 1864 Act applied to specific named naval ports and garrison towns. It allowed the police to arrest prostitutes and order them to undergo an

internal examination. If they were infected with venereal disease, they were detained until they were cured. If a woman refused, she could be thrown into prison after a trial in which she had to prove she was virtuous.

2 The 1866 Act extended the 1864 Act in that prostitutes in naval ports and garrison towns were subject to compulsory three-monthly internal examinations; regular examinations of suspected prostitutes within ten miles of the named ports and garrison towns were introduced.

3 The 1869 Act extended the 1866 Act to all garrison towns and allowed suspected prostitutes to be locked up for five days before they were examined.

The government saw the Acts as a means of maintaining military efficiency; the medical profession as a means of stamping out a debilitating illness; and many ordinary people as a moral duty and even an act of kindness to the prostitutes.

In practice, however, the implementation of the Acts was crude, insensitive and degrading. For example, in the Devonport dockyards the internal examination of prostitutes was watched through windows by jeering dockyard workers. It was also very difficult, in borderline cases, for the police to determine who was, or was not, a prostitute. Many innocent women and young people were arrested and medically examined. Some lost their jobs as a result and even committed suicide.

But the attempt in the autumn of 1869 to extend the provisions of the Contagious Diseases Acts to all prostitutes everywhere in the land created uproar.

Women go on the offensive

On 1 January 1870, one hundred and forty respectable, middle- and upper-class women, many of whom were well known for their literary, religious and charitable works, signed a manifesto protesting against the Contagious Diseases Acts. Amongst the signatures were those of Florence Nightingale (see page 5), **Lydia Becker** (see page 52) and, significantly, **Josephine Butler** (see page 27). The signatories declared that the Acts removed security from women and put their reputations in the hands of the police. Furthermore, they emphasised the injustice of punishing prostitutes but not the men who used and abused them. This was sensational stuff! There was an outcry of shocked hostility, not only because women had dared to organise and protest in this manner, but also because they had gone public on such a taboo subject.

In 1869 these women had formed the Ladies' National Association (LNA), headed up by Josephine Butler. This was to be the hub of a nationwide campaign to repeal the Contagious Diseases Acts. The majority of the LNA's national leaders were experienced in radical politics; most came from families who had been involved in the political agitations of the 1830s and 1840s when pressure for the reform of parliament and the abolition of

Source M

One MP said to me, 'We know how to manage any other opposition in the House or in the country, but this is very awkward for us – this revolt of the women. It is quite a new thing; what are we to do with such an opposition as this?'

From Josephine Butler *Personal Reminiscences of a Great Crusade* published in 1896

SKILLS BUILDER

What can you learn from this poster about the campaign to repeal the Contagious Diseases Acts?

Discuss this in your group and draw up a list, with the evidence to support what you think.

the Corn Laws was at an all-time high. However, the idea that the Contagious Diseases Acts were barbaric and demeaning quickly gained currency throughout the country. Before long, every major city had repeal committees comprising both men and women, and many had 'women only' sub-committees. This organised protest, led by women and on such a subject, was completely unprecedented. Although few realised it at the time, it was to be the shape of things to come.

Indeed. This was the question, asked in Source M, that was to reverberate down through the years, as women grew more and more vocal in demanding their rights.

Source N

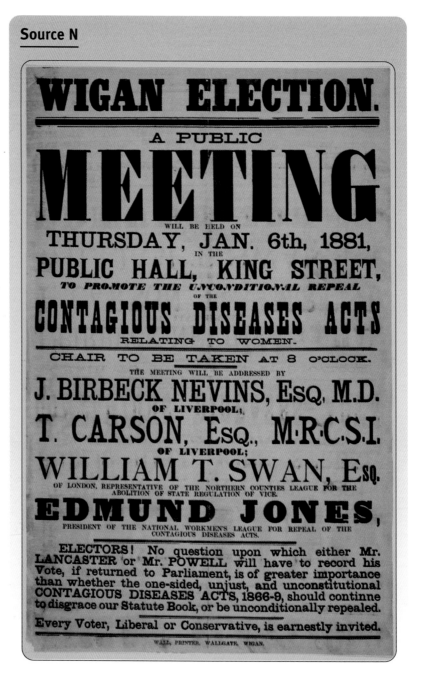

2.4 A Wigan election poster, 1881

Strategy and tactics

The strategy and tactics used by Josephine Butler and her supporters were to form the template for all future protest groups. There were letters and petitions, mass meetings and protest marches. They discovered that an effective method was to target specific parliamentary candidates. One such candidate was Sir Henry Storks, who had been selected by the Liberals for the parliamentary seat of Newark. He happened, unfortunately for him, to support the Contagious Diseases Acts and had supported their implementation there with great gusto. The poster and placard campaign organised in Newark against him was so intense that he withdrew his candidature. A different, pro-repeal candidate was selected and elected in his place. Storks then applied for the relatively safe seat of Colchester. Again, an intense poster and placard campaign against him was severely damaging. It split the Liberal vote and allowed the Tories to take the seat. The suffragettes were to learn from this.

And finally . . .

Following a highly successful campaign that didn't lose momentum, the Contagious Diseases Acts were repealed in 1886.

Source O

Josephine Butler fundamentally changed the terms of women's political lives. She not only challenged the Victorian taboo that sexual matters were unmentionable, but, by taking a dominant role in a major pressure group, permanently destroyed the notion that women could not take a leading part in politics.

From T. Fisher 'Josephine Butler: feminism's neglected pioneer' in *History Today* Vol. 46.6 published in June 1996

Biography

Josephine Butler 1828–1906

Josephine was born into a wealthy landowning family in Northumberland. Her father, John Grey:

- was the cousin of Earl Grey who led the Whig government when parliament passed the Reform Act of 1832;
- played a leading part in advocating parliamentary reform and the repeal of the Corn Laws;
- campaigned against the slave trade;
- was a strong believer in social reform.

Josephine, therefore, grew up in a family with strong views about the wrongs of inequality and injustice and the need for social reform. In 1852 she married George Butler, an academic, who had similar views to her. They had four children. In 1863 Josephine watched helplessly as their youngest child and only daughter, Eva, fell to her death from a balcony when she was six years old. This greatly affected Josephine, and for the rest of her life she was to focus on helping women and young girls because they were 'someone's daughter'. She:

- worked with Anne Jemima Clough to establish educational courses for women and in 1867 was appointed president of the North of England Council for the Higher Education of Women;
- became involved, in 1868, in a campaign to persuade Cambridge University to allow women to be University students;
- wrote *The Education and Employment of Women* in 1868 in which she argued that there should be better and more opportunities in education and employment for single women;
- wrote *Women's Work and Women's Culture* in 1869 in which she argued that women should not try to compete with men on the same terms because they were different – equal, but different. She applied this argument to female suffrage: women should have the vote because they were different from men and had different strengths to offer society;
- worked as leader of the Ladies' National Association from 1869, which successfully campaigned for the repeal of the Contagious Diseases Acts;
- became involved in the campaign against child prostitution, which resulted in the 1885 Criminal Amendment Act that raised the age of consent from thirteen to sixteen;
- supported the National Union of Suffrage Societies that campaigned peacefully for female suffrage.

Unit summary

What have you learned in this unit?

By the end of the nineteenth century, considerable progress had been made in enabling married women to gain some sort of control over their personal lives. They could retain the property and money they brought with them into the marriage; divorce was easier and access and even custody of the children of the marriage was made possible. There was, however, a long way to go before husbands and wives were seen legally as equal partners within a marriage.

The campaign to repeal the Contagious Diseases Acts was yet another way of trying to give women control over their lives. The repeal of the Acts meant that prostitutes were no longer subject to intrusive internal examinations at the whim of a police officer. Those women who worked on the campaign were exhibiting a freedom never before experienced and they set a template for all future campaigns.

What skills have you used in this unit?

You have used the skill of empathy to begin to understand why the Victorians seemed to have double standards of sexual morality and how this impacted on men's attitude to legislation concerning women's rights and freedoms. You have applied this understanding to an evaluation of the relevant source material.

SKILLS BUILDER

1 Work in a group.

   Go back to Source A. It is a narrative painting, which means that the picture tells a story. But in this case, the picture tells the end of the story. What was the whole story? How did it begin? Remember to keep to the context of the time.

2 Look at Sources G, K and N.

   How useful are cartoons and posters as evidence of attitudes at the time?

3 Work in pairs.

   You must decide whether Caroline Norton or Josephine Butler brought about greater changes in women's personal lives in this period.

   One of you should work on Caroline and the other on Josephine. Make out a case.

   Present your case either orally or via a PowerPoint presentation.

   Vote as a group. Who wins? Why?

Exam tips

This is the sort of question you will find appearing on examination papers in a (b) question.

4 Study Sources F, G and H and use your own knowledge.
   Do you agree with the view that, by 1882, the concept of the 'angel in the house' had been overturned?

- **Do** be clear about the question focus – what is being claimed? In this case, what is being claimed is that the 'angel in the house' concept had been overturned by 1882.
- **Analyse** the sources to establish points that support and points that challenge the view given in the question.
- **Develop** each point by reference to your own wider knowledge, using it to reinforce and/or challenge the points derived from the sources.
- **Combine** the points into arguments for and against the stated view.
- **Evaluate** the conflicting arguments.
- Present a **judgement** as to the validity of the stated view.

And above all, **plan** your answer.

Start now by using the exam tips to draw up a plan that would deliver an answer to this question (question 4). You might find that using a spider diagram would be the best way to do this.

RESEARCH TASK

Elizabeth Wolstenholme Elmy (1834–1913)

How significant was the contribution made by Elizabeth Wolstenholme Elmy to changing people's attitudes to a woman's place within marriage?

3 To what extent did women become involved in public life before 1901?

What is this unit about?

This unit focuses on the ways in which women participated in public life in the last half of the nineteenth century. Although legislation enabling them to do this is important, the emphasis in this unit will be on what women actually did and the impact they had on their communities. In it you will:

- find out how women contributed to the administration of the Poor Law, the running of schools and the development of political parties;
- assess the impact women had on public life in the last half of the nineteenth century.

Key questions

- Why were only some aspects of public life deemed appropriate fields in which women could contribute?
- How far did women's limited involvement in public life create additional pressure for the vote?

Timeline

1859	The Workhouse Visiting Society founded
1869	Municipal Franchise Act allows unmarried women ratepayers to vote in municipal elections
1870	Education Act allows women ratepayers to vote for, and serve on, the new school boards
1875	First women elected to serve on Poor Law Boards as guardians of the poor
1881	First Women's Liberal Association formed in Bristol
1883	Primrose League established
1887	Women's Liberal Foundation established
1894	Local Government Act gave married women the right to vote in local elections and allowed women to stand for election as municipal councillors

Source A

JUNE 14, 1884.]   PUNCH, OR THE LONDON CHARIVARI.   279

"THE ANGEL IN 'THE HOUSE;'" OR, THE RESULT OF FEMALE SUFFRAGE.
(*A Troubled Dream of the Future.*)

3.1 A cartoon published in the magazine *Punch* in June 1884

SKILLS BUILDER

1 What is this cartoonist's attitude to women?
2 How do you think this attitude affected women trying to contribute to public life?

The vote!

No – not that one! That had to wait until 1918. But some women achieved the right to vote in local government elections long before they had the right to vote in national elections. Source B explains why this was.

Source B

Positions in local government (on School Boards, as Poor Law guardians or as local councillors) could be interpreted as an extension of women's caring role within the family, but remained less prestigious than similar work done by men.

From S. D'Cruze *Women and the Family* published in 1995

So women were beginning, on a small scale, to gain a foothold in political life, but it remained a man's world where the contribution of men, even if identical, was to be valued above that of women. Nevertheless, in 1869 single and widowed women who paid rates were given the right to vote in local elections; married women had to wait until the 1894 Local Government Act.

What impact did women have on children's lives when serving on school boards?

It was the Education Act of 1870 that first allowed women to stand for election to school boards and so begin to have an impact on the lives of children beyond those in their immediate family.

Why was an Education Act necessary in 1870?

Before 1870, education was not provided by the state, but through a mixture of voluntary organisations, charitable institutions and the churches. Education was not compulsory and huge areas of the country were without any schools of any sort at all. About 34 per cent of children aged between six and twelve did not receive any education at all. The situation was worsened by:

- the rapid population growth;
- the concentration of this population in industrialised and industrialising towns, where the existing provision simply couldn't cope.

There was also a perception that an illiterate, innumerate workforce would lead to Britain falling behind her industrial competitors such as Germany and the USA. What brought matters to a head was the 1867 Reform Act that gave the vote to working-class men in the towns.

'It will be absolutely necessary to educate our masters' said the Liberal politician Robert Lowe, 'You have placed the government of this country in the hands of the masses.'

What was a school board?

In 1870, the Liberal MP for Bradford, W.E. Forster, persuaded parliament to provide elementary education for all. His Education Act divided England into districts and set up elementary schools in those districts where there were few elementary schools or none at all. Existing voluntary, charitable and church-run schools were not abolished, and so a dual system operated in the country with the state-funded schools plugging the gaps in the existing provision.

School boards were elected to run the districts into which the country was divided and women could stand for election to these school boards. Women could also work voluntarily as managers of individual schools. So women had a very real opportunity to make a difference at both a local and regional level.

Source C

A recognised lady member, if not two, upon the managing committee [school board] of every elementary school in the country, would be of the greatest advantage to the schools, to the teacher, and to the Department [of Education]. Women are slow to see their duty in these matters, and sometimes seem to think it more feminine to shrink from a definite position, preferring the greater and, as it seems to them, less fettered liberty of desultory action.

From Duties of Women as School Managers by Louisa Hubbard published in 1878. Louisa was an author, editor and strong supporter of working women and their rights. Here she sets out to persuade women to become school managers.

Louisa Hubbard continues by describing how a woman can contribute to the education of children by working voluntarily as school managers:

The duties which fall to the share of school managers are simple, and require common sense and a real sympathy with the teacher and the children more than any special gifts. A lady can probably enter into the difficulties of the locality and of the home associations of the children, their social and family circumstances, and be on terms of greater intimacy with the teachers, than is possible for any man, or, at any rate, of the busy men of whom such committees are generally composed. If our schools are to be places of education, if they are to be schools of morality as well as places of instruction, questions arise which require wise and delicate handling, and need the united efforts and the fullest mutual confidence between the managers and teachers to deal properly with them.

There are two departments of school work in which teachers, almost without exception, will warmly welcome assistance; and this would therefore seem naturally to fall to the share of the lady manager – help in teaching the needlework, and some extra instruction afforded to the pupil-teachers. Managers may do great good by taking classes in needlework and cutting out, provided they do so regularly and in subordination to the school timetable. Much valuable assistance may be given out of school hours in helping the teachers prepare the work. A lady may also give useful help by taking the reading lesson. She may also look up absentees, and provide for proper precautions when infectious illness is discovered among the children.

But it is with respect to the moral condition of the school and its influences upon the children for good or for evil that the lady manager will be of most service.

SKILLS BUILDER

How does Louisa explain why some women may not have been too keen on getting themselves elected to school boards? Does she approve of their 'excuses' or not?

Question

To what extent would a strong supporter of the 'angel in the house' and 'separate spheres' philosophies find it acceptable for women to serve on school boards? Discuss this in your group.

Source D

The Committee on School Accommodation and Attendance has to enforce the by-laws dealing with attendance at school of all the children, including the blind, deaf, difficult and crippled children; it watches the growth and shifting of population, and decides on the districts in which additional school provision is needed, and decides where a new site should be acquired or an old one disposed of; it also watches all Bills in parliament which affect the Board's work, and conducts most of the Board's correspondence with the Education Department.

Miss Davenport Hill and Mrs Homan were on this committee.

From *Women on School Boards* written by Florence Davenport Hill in 1896. Florence was a social reformer and strong supporter of women's suffrage. Here she is writing about the work of the London school board committees.

For some women and some men, politics and education were inextricably mixed. In 1894, members of the Bradford branch of the newly formed Independent Labour Party (ILP) invited Margaret McMillan to the city in order to help establish the party as a political force in the town. One of the ways in which she was able to do this was by standing for election to the Bradford School Board.

Source E

Standing as an ILP representative for the Bradford School Board, she [Margaret McMillan] was elected, the only woman member, in November 1894. It was here that the real battle began. It was a battle not only against ignorance, complacency and pomposity, but also against the vested interest of the conservative/**denominational** group of men who dominated the School Board.

'How can we,' Margaret McMillan was to ask a startled School Board, 'educate dirty, hungry and ailing children?' She fought long and hard to have baths built in Wapping Road School. Her eventual victory brought about change in the constitution and attitude of the Board, and enabled her to continue her battle for the slum child with less opposition. The provision of baths in one school was followed by the building of baths in others; medical inspections were instituted; a school clinic established; hungry children were fed.

From Rosemary Rees *Social and Political Change in England: Margaret McMillan and the Battle for the Slum Child* published in 1986

Definition

Denominational

Connected to one of the branches of the Christian church.

Question

Read Sources D and E. Do you think Margaret McMillan or Miss Davenport Hill and Mrs Holman had the greater impact on the education of children?

It is clear that women did play an important part on school boards and committees, and as managers of individual schools. However, this was not to last. In 1902, Local Authorities replaced School Boards and women were declared ineligible for election. The administration of education had suddenly become too important to allow women to take a share (see page 132).

How important was women's involvement in Poor Law administration?

There was no actual law preventing women from becoming **Poor Law guardians** provided they owned enough property, but it seems that they did not move officially into this field of public service until towards the end of the century. The first woman was elected to be a Poor Law guardian in 1875 and this seemed to open the floodgates. By 1901 there were about 1,000 female guardians of the poor, distributed throughout some 500 poor law unions. But before this official involvement, many women were doing what they could to improve conditions in Britain's workhouses.

Christmas Day in the workhouse

The marriage of Queen Victoria to Prince Albert in 1840 resulted, among other things, in the introduction of Germanic customs at Christmas. The Victorians discovered Christmas: Christmas trees, Christmas presents, and Charles Dickens wrote *A Christmas Carol*. This was not lost on those who administered the Poor Law, and even the Poor Law Board, who took office in 1847, authorised all guardians to provide 'treats' for workhouse inmates at Christmas time. Curiously, many guardians interpreted this as providing 'treats' for adults only. Workhouse children were frequently ignored. In 1837, the Chairman of Petworth guardians was asked by a parliamentary committee 'Supposing any charitable lady in the neighbourhood was desirous of giving the children a dinner on Christmas Day, could you, as Chairman of the Board, allow a thing of that sort to be done?' The reply was 'No, I could not.' He was not alone, and it was because of attitudes like this that women began to intervene.

> **Definition**
>
> **Poor Law guardian**
>
> All workhouses had guardians. These were people elected by the local community to make sure they were run properly.

Source F

We wrote to our friends in the county town near, to ask for contributions, saying that headless horses, eyeless dolls, wheel-less wagons and nursery rubbish would be acceptable. We spent ten shillings on dolls, marbles, tops, begged at our draper's for scraps of material . . . On Christmas Eve we drove up to the workhouse, carrying baskets of toys. The girls' school first – spiritless, cowed, sad looking girls, aged from three to sixteen years old . . . we gladdened every little heart of the sixty girls by some trifle given into their own hands. Then to the boys' school where I was all but pushed over with the eagerness of the fine lads. One liked to see their joy in the presents, forgetful for the time of pauper clothing, pauper food and pauper imprisonment. To the baby nursery next, where every crib was made happy by a hairless, legless horse or a stump of a doll – something to hold and love. On, on to the sick children's ward, where into every bed we slipped a fully dressed doll. The little weary eyes closed as the arms enfolded the future companion of its solitude; no more dreary nights 'dolly would be there'; no more dreary days 'dolly would be talked to'.

From an article written by Mrs Emma Sheppard of Frome, Somerset, published in a Bristol newspaper in 1854. Here she explains how she and her children brought Christmas cheer to some workhouse children.

Emma Sheppard's article was re-printed many times in a number of pamphlets under increasingly sentimental titles such as *Sunshine in a Shady Place* and rapidly became a bestseller. Other middle-class mothers quickly followed suit and published their accounts of how they attempted to bring some Christmas joy to youngsters in the workhouses.

Source G

We began with the nursery where the babies and children under three years old are kept. It was a cheerless sight enough, though the room was large and airy, and clean as whitewash could make it, and the babies – there were about thirty altogether – showed no signs of ill-usage or neglect. But it was the unnatural stillness of the little things that affected me painfully. All remained perfectly grave and noiseless, even when the basket of toys was brought in. There was no jumping up, no shouting, no eager demand for some particularly noisy or gaudy plaything. They held out their tiny hands, and took the toys when they were bid, just looked at them listlessly for a minute and then lapsed into quiet dullness again, equally regardless of the ladies' simulated expressions of delight and surprise, or the good clergyman's exhortation to them to 'be good children and deserve all the pretty things the kind ladies gave them'. I saw only two children who looked really pleased and understood how to play with the toys given them; and they, I was told, had only been in the workhouse a few days.

From an article in *Macmillan's Magazine* written by a middle-class mother and published in 1861

SKILLS BUILDER

Why do you think there is such a difference between these two accounts?

It is easy to be cynical and to see these women as trying to outdo each other in their charity and to view what they did as being patronising in the extreme. But whatever their motives and method of delivery, they did make a beginning in persuading the authorities to understand that toys and private possessions were essential to a child's development.

The Workhouse Visiting Society 1859

The unofficial opening of some workhouses to visitors like Emma Sheppard began in 1850, and was formally recognised in 1857. However, it was not until 1859 that visiting became nationally organised due to the drive and determination of **Louisa Twining** (see page 37). The newly formed Workhouse Visiting Society had a committee that comprised sixty-three highly respectable citizens: doctors and lawyers, the wives of politicians, clergymen, including four bishops, and twelve members of the aristocracy.

So respectable, in fact, that they were not suspected of having radical, reforming intentions. But Louisa had chosen wisely. The committee became the spearhead for workhouse reform. The overt aim of the Society was to bring help and comfort to individual paupers; its covert aim was to influence public opinion in order to bring about a national change of attitude to the poor and to the causes of poverty.

Biography

Louisa Twining 1820–1912

Louisa, the youngest of eight children, was born into a comfortable middle-class family, who owned a tea- and coffee-importing business. As a child, she was encouraged to think of others less privileged than herself, and regularly visited the poor in cottages near her brothers' school, Rugby. As an adult, she regularly visited the poor living in hovels close to the Twining's London home in the Strand. She was a talented artist and in 1852, published a book called *Symbols and Emblems of Early and Medieval Art*. The following year, however, her life was to take quite a different direction. She was refused permission by the guardians to visit a former nurse she had befriended and who had been forced to enter the Strand workhouse; an interview with the President of the Poor Law Board achieved nothing, and Louisa began what was to become a lifetime's work. She:

- visited any workhouse that would let her in;
- bombarded the press with letters and wrote numerous pamphlets about workhouse conditions and Poor Law policy;
- was allowed in 1857 to set up the first visiting committee as a result of two pamphlets *Practical Lectures to Ladies* and *A Few Words about the Inmates of our Union Workhouses* and a petition;
- set up, in 1859, the Workhouse Visiting Society that published its journal from 1859–1865 and was active in workhouse reform;
- helped establish, in 1861, a home for workhouse girls who were then sent out into domestic service;
- called for women Poor Law inspectors and for workhouse girls to be given a training in a trade, which led to Mrs Nassau Senior being appointed the first female Inspector in 1872;
- gave classes for women at the Working Men's College;
- became involved with the Society for Promoting the Employment of women;
- worked as a Poor Law guardian between 1884 and 1890 for the Kensington union workhouse;
- retired to Worthing in 1890 where she organised a system of district nursing;
- moved to Tunbridge Wells where in the years 1893–6 she started a children's nursery and became Poor Law guardian of the Tunbridge Union workhouse.

Source H

I found old folks sitting on backless forms or benches. They had no privacy, no possessions, not even a locker. The old women were without pockets in their gowns so they were obliged to keep any poor little treasures they had in their bosoms. Soon after I took office we gave the old people comfortable Windsor chairs to sit in, and in a number of ways we managed to make their existence more endurable.

From Emmeline Pankhurst *My Own Story* published in 1914. Here she is describing one aspect of her work as a Poor Law guardian in Manchester in 1895.

Question

Emmeline Pankhurst (see page 80) was writing many years after the formation of the Workhouse Visiting Society. Does this mean that the Society's work was unsuccessful?

How active were women in politics before 1901?

The widening of the **franchise** in the third Reform Act of 1884 doubled the number of men eligible to vote from nearly 3 million to 6 million. Whereas before 1884, one man in three had the vote, after 1884 the ratio rose to two men in every three. The Act also restructured the constituencies. In order to ensure the support of the new voters was captured and that of old supporters was retained, the political parties had to get themselves organised. This is where they turned to the women, and where women gained experience of national parties and national politics.

Source I

Since Gladstone's legislation against corrupt electoral practices set limits on campaign expenditures, volunteers were needed to supplement the services of paid agents. Thus a perfect opportunity was at hand to engage the legions of women eager to help friends and relatives who were campaigning for office.

From C. Hirshfield 'Fractured Faith: Liberal Party Women and the Suffrage Issue in Britain 1892–1914' published in *Gender and History* Volume 2.2 Summer 1990

Once again, women were seen in a supporting role. The 'friends and relatives' campaigning for office were, of course, men. However, one consequence of the widening of the franchise was the growth of women's political organisations.

The Conservative Party and the Primrose League

The Primrose League was set up in 1883 to promote the Conservative Party and to support aspiring Tory members of parliament. Unsurprisingly, its membership was strictly hierarchical: there was one class of membership with an expensive subscription, favoured by the upper classes, and a cheaper, associate membership, favoured by the lower classes. What it did do, though, was to admit men and women on equal terms. Historian Martin Pugh has analysed the early membership records.

Source J

They obviously corroborate the impressionistic evidence of the Primrose League as an organisation which catered to women: but what is more striking is that they show the League as a body which incorporated men and women rather than segregating them. Moreover, they suggest that the Primrose League – uniquely for a Victorian political institution – must have included hundreds of thousands of women in its ranks.

From Martin Pugh *The Tories and the People 1880–1935* published in 1985

Local Primrose League groups were called 'habitations' and within these habitations, women were heavily involved on the social side, organising fetes and garden parties and other such fund-raising events. On the political side, they delivered leaflets and helped bring Conservative voters in to the polls on election days. Again, a supportive but very necessary role.

Source K

The most impressive feature of this great meeting was the presence of hundreds of women who were not there, as they would have been in a political meeting almost everywhere in the United States, on sufferance. They were a component part, a vital factor, in what today is one of the greatest political organisations in England; officers, delegates, equal in authority with men. Fully a third of them – every woman householder – were entitled to vote at all except the parliamentary elections, and they constituted what Liberal and Conservatives alike recognised and, what is more, respected – an active political influence which both parties were forced to accept as such.

An American, Mary H. Krout, was a guest in 1896 at the annual Habitation of the Primrose League. This was a very grand affair, held in the Covent Garden Opera House. Lord Salisbury was the guest speaker and all the local Primrose League habitations sent delegates. Mary wrote about her experiences as a visitor to London in *A Looker-on in London* published in 1899. This is part of what she said about the 1896 annual Habitation.

Questions

How far do you think Mary Krout's enthusiasm for what she saw at the Primrose League's annual habitation was partly because of the contrast it made with what would have happened in the USA?

There is a tremendous contradiction in Mary Krout's account. Can you spot it?

The Primrose League did not campaign on behalf of women's suffrage. Many of its members were suffragists but they were not able to influence the policy of the Ladies Grand Council, which was that members were free to support votes for women but that it was not and never would be one of the policy aims of the Primrose League.

Question

How might members of the Ladies Grand Council have supported this position?

The Liberal Party and the Women's Liberal Association

Although the first Women's Liberal Association was formed (in Bristol) in 1881, it wasn't until the obvious success of the Primrose League that the idea of women's associations began to take a hold. In 1887 the different associations all came together under the umbrella Women's Liberal Federation. This had a council of 500 delegates elected by the local associations and an executive committee of thirty, elected by the council. Unlike the Primrose League, the women's Liberal associations operated separately from the all-male local associations, yet they fulfilled the same functions as the women in the Primrose League. C. Hirshfield is quoted again in Source L (see page 40).

Source L

The main function of the WLAs was to carry out canvassing and other political work (such as leafleting and encouraging voters to register). Although it was usually the wives, mothers and daughters of prominent politicians who established local Liberal associations, the Women's Liberal Federation attempted from the start to broaden its membership base, often seeking to enlist professional women and veterans of the temperance and moral reform movements. As a result, WLAs often provided grass-roots support for people anxious to seek office at both the local and national level. Liberal women learned not only to face the general public in door-to-door canvassing, but also to confront male politicians in local meetings. Inevitably, they were introduced to the techniques of practical electioneering, and many learned their lesson well.

From C. Hirshfield 'Fractured Faith: Liberal Party Women and the Suffrage Issue in Britain 1892–1914' published in *Gender and History* Volume 2.2 Summer 1990

Question

Was there any real difference between the activities of the Primrose League and the Women's Liberal Associations?

Local councils and women

The 1894 Local Government Act not only gave married women the right to join single-women and widowed-women ratepayers in voting in local elections, it also allowed women to stand for election as municipal councillors. Many did, and when elected could face a fairly difficult time as the only woman councillor on a male-dominated council, not all members of which welcomed her presence. Nevertheless, the women persisted and, almost inevitably, concerned themselves with welfare issues. For example:

- Eleanor Rathbone, on Liverpool City Council, involved herself in pushing for improved housing for the poor.
- Susan Lawrence, on the London County Council, worked on the Education Committee but also fought for the rights of women cleaners who were being abused by male caretakers. She was to join the Labour Party and hold a post in the first Labour government of 1924.
- Margaret Ashton became the first woman to sit on Manchester City Council. Here, her activities were wide and varied, ranging from founding the local Woman's Trade Union council to setting up a babies' hospital in Burnage. A suffragette sympathiser, she used her councillor status to make her views clear on votes for women, health and education.
- Nettie Adler, the daughter of the Chief Rabbi, represented Hackney on the London County Council where she worked to reduce child labour and concerned herself with the status of women industrial workers. She was to be appointed a Justice of the Peace (JP) and worked on the Shoreditch Juvenile Court.

Questions

- What skills do you think women would have gained by their involvement in political life?
- To what extent do you think this involvement would have encouraged women to believe that they were entitled to the vote on the same terms as men? Debate this in your group.

Now read what Baroness Patricia Hollis had to say.

Source M

Women believed that such local government work would win them the vote. However, Liberals feared that propertied women would vote Tory; Tories, that female suffrage would challenge male authority. Gladstone added that if married women got the vote, husbands would either have two votes or engage in marital dispute; yet if votes were confined to spinsters and widows, they would be rewarding those without a husband, the failures of their sex. So clearly you couldn't enfranchise any women. The Lords thought this argument very fetching.

Indeed, far from local government being a stepping stone to the vote, it blocked it. Men now decided that there were two spheres of politics: the domestic – education, poor law, hospital work, which women could and should do; and imperial – war, commerce, empire, finance, which women clearly could not. Precisely because women found their appropriate service in local government, they were not needed, or wanted, at Westminster. As the Archbishop of Canterbury said, trying, but perhaps failing, to be helpful in the 1907 debate, it was women's service that was needed, not women's rights.

From a speech made by Baroness Patricia Hollis to the AGM of the Women's Local Government Society in Sheffield Town Hall on 10 March 2007

Unit summary

What have you learned in this unit?

By the end of the nineteenth century, middle-class women were involved in public life to a considerable extent. If they were unmarried and ratepayers, they were allowed to vote in municipal elections. Married or unmarried, women could work in a voluntary capacity on school boards and as guardians of the poor. This was considered by most men to be an appropriate extension of their domestic role. Following the 1867 Reform Act, women became more involved in national politics because the increased male electorate meant that the political parties needed the organisational skills that women were willing to provide voluntarily. Because all of this involvement in public life was unpaid, it only attracted those women who had private incomes or whose husband's supported them and were willing for them to become so involved.

What skills have you used in this unit?

You will have understood the limitations on women's ability to participate in public life and the varied reasons for those limitations. In addressing the reasons for the limitations, you have made links between them and cross-referenced to the attitudes explored in Units 1 and 2.

SKILLS BUILDER

1 Think about Source A. How would you argue (a) that the cartoonist is right and (b) that the cartoonist is wrong? Work in pairs.

2 How far does the evidence suggest that women were effective in ameliorating the worse effects of the Poor Law?

3 Put all the women mentioned in this unit in an imaginary balloon. Organise a balloon debate, matching a student with each woman, and with the student speaking out in defence of his/her chosen woman. Who is left in the balloon? Why?

Exam tips

This is the sort of question you will find appearing on the examination paper as an (a) question.

Read Sources F, G and H.

How far does Source H challenge the effectiveness of women's work in administering the Poor Law described in Sources F and G?

You tackled an (a) type question at the end of Unit 1. Look back at the Exam Tips you were given there on page 10. Now is the time to consolidate those tips. What do you have to do to write a successful answer to an (a) type question?

- get underneath the sources and make **inferences** from them.
- **compare** the sources by analysing their similarities and differences.
- **contextualise** the sources, giving weight to the significance of their origin, nature and purpose.
- reach a judgement on 'how far' by using the sources as a set.

Remember, there is the Exam zone section at the end of the book to help you further.

Now plan an answer to this question and write a response.

RESEARCH TASK

The Independent Labour Party (ILP)

You read that Margaret McMillan was a member of the ILP.

- When did the ILP start and who was its founder?

- What was the main aim of the ILP?

- What was the ILP's attitude to the role of women in public life?

4 Suffragists: getting started c.1860–c.1903

What is this unit about?

This unit focuses on the ways in which the belief that women should be enfranchised developed into a full-scale national campaign. In this unit you will:

- find out how men and women started the campaign for female suffrage;
- work with source material to evaluate the nature of the campaign and the reasons why it started.

Key questions

- Why did a national campaign for female suffrage begin?
- How did men and women contribute to the early suffragist campaigns?

Timeline

1865	Election of John Stuart Mill as an MP
1866	Women's Suffrage Committee founded in London Manchester National Society for Women's Suffrage founded with Lydia Becker as its secretary
1867	Second Reform Act
1868	Leeds *Express* publishes Sarah Ann Jackson's poem Lily Maxwell and nine other Manchester women vote in the general election
1870	*Punch* publishes cartoon 'An Ugly Rush' Richard Pankhurst drafts and introduces to parliament the first Women's Suffrage bill
1872	National Society for Women's Suffrage combines local women's suffrage groups
1889	Formation of Women's Franchise League with Emmeline Pankhurst as its leader An Appeal against Female Suffrage signed by over 100 mostly titled women
1894	Local Government Act
1897	Faithful Begg MP presents a Women's Suffrage bill to parliament Formation of National Union of Women's Suffrage Societies with Millicent Fawcett as its president

Source A

4.1 This cartoon, called 'An Ugly Rush', was published in the magazine *Punch* in May 1870

At first sight, it doesn't seem as if the women's suffrage movement got off to a particularly good start! John Bull (representing the average Englishman) is leaning hard against the door that would have let women in to enjoy the privileges of the right to vote.

SKILLS BUILDER

- Is the cartoonist in favour of women's suffrage, or not? What evidence have you used in reaching your conclusion?
- What are the women and little girl on the far right doing? What point was the cartoonist making when he drew them there?

What was the nature of the debate about women's suffrage?

Before looking at the beginnings of the women's suffrage movement, it is sensible to look first at the reasons why women wanted the vote and at the reasons why people opposed women having the vote. If female suffrage was to be attained, the arguments of those opposing it had to be destroyed.

What were the arguments in favour of women having the vote?

It would be best to let the women speak for themselves. As you read through these next sources, think not only about the reasons the different women are giving for wanting the vote, but also about the time they were writing.

Source B

It seems to me that while a Reform Bill [which became the 1867 Reform Act] is under discussion and petitions are being presented to parliament from various classes, it is very desirable that women who wish for political enfranchisement should say so. I think the most important thing is to make a demand and commence the first humble beginnings of an agitation for which reasons can be given that are in harmony with the political ideas of English people in general. No idea is so universally accepted and acceptable in England as that taxation and representation ought to go together, and people in general will be much more willing to listen to the assertion that single widows and widows of property have been unjustly overlooked and left out from the privileges to which their property entitles them, than to the much more startling general proposition that sex is not a proper ground of distinction in political rights.

Part of a letter from Helen Taylor to Barbara Bodichon, written on 9 May 1866. Barbara Bodichon (see page 22) and Helen Taylor were active in the women's suffrage campaign.

It may well be that widow Sarah Ann Jackson put the case much more succinctly in 1868, quoted in Source C.

Source C

I wonder, Mr Editor,
Why I can't have the vote;
And I will not be contented
Till I've found the reason out.
I am a working woman.
My voting half is dead.
I hold a house and want to know
Why I can't vote instead.
I pay my rates in person,
Under protest tho' 'tis true;
But I pay them, and am qualified
To vote as well as you.

Part of a poem written by Sarah Ann Jackson published in the *Leeds Express* on 4 March 1868

Source D

With regard to the differences between men and women, those who advocate the enfranchisement of women have no wish to disregard them or make little of them. On the contrary, we base our claim to representation to a large extent on them. If men and women were exactly alike, the representation of men would represent us; but not being alike, that wherein we differ is unrepresented under the present system.

But this difference between men and women, instead of being a reason against their enfranchisement, seems to me the strongest possible reason in favour of it; we want the home and the domestic side of things to count for more in politics and in the administrations of public affairs than they do at present. We want to know how various kinds of legislative enactments bear on the home and domestic life. And we want to force our legislators to consider the domestic as well as the political results of any legislation which many of them are advocating.

I advocate the extension of the franchise to women because I wish to strengthen true womanliness in woman, and because I want to see the womanly and domestic side of things weigh more and count more in all public concerns.

From Millicent Fawcett in a pamphlet *Home and Politics*; date of publication unknown

Source E

We wish for it [the vote] because there exits a terrible trade of procuring young girls for immoral purposes. The girl is first entrapped and seduced, and when once she has fallen, it is very difficult for her to return afterwards to her home, or to be received among respectable girls in workshops or in domestic service. She becomes a prostitute.

We believe the time has come when women must claim their right to help and the first steps to this lies in their enfranchisement, for without this they have no real power in the matter. It would be much more difficult for this cruel and wicked traffic to be carried on if it were recognised by the law that women were of the same value and had the same standing in the state as men.

From a leading member of the National Union of Women's Suffrage Societies (NUWSS) at the beginning of the twentieth century

SKILLS BUILDER

- What different reasons are suggested here as reasons for enfranchising women?
- Sources D and E have incomplete attributions. We do not know when Source D was written and we do not know exactly who wrote Source E, nor exactly when it was written. Does this matter?

Source F

Why Women Want the Vote

BECAUSE no race or class or sex can have its interest properly safeguarded in the legislature of a country unless it is represented by direct suffrage

BECAUSE while men who are voters can get their economic grievances listened to, non-voters are disregarded

BECAUSE politics and economics go hand in hand. And so long as woman has no political status she will be the 'bottom dog' as a wage earner

BECAUSE the legislature in the past has not made laws which are equal between men and women: and these laws will not be altered until women get the vote

BECAUSE all the more important and lucrative positions are barred to them, and opportunities of public service are denied

BECAUSE wherever women have become voters, reform has proceeded more rapidly than before, and even at home, our municipal government in which the women have a certain share, is in advance and not behind our parliamentary attitude on many important questions

BECAUSE women will be better comrades to their husbands, better mothers to their children, and better housekeepers of the home.

From a leaflet produced by the NUWSS in 1907

Questions

- Which of the reasons for emancipating women given in Source F do you find the most convincing?
- Which of the reasons do you think people at the time would have found the most convincing?

Biography

Millicent Garrett (1847–1929)

Millicent (Garrett) Fawcett after 1867

Millicent was born in Aldeburgh, Suffolk, the seventh of ten children of an East Anglian corn and coal merchant. One of her sisters was Elizabeth Garrett Anderson (see page 142). Millicent had no formal schooling except for three years at a school in Blackheath, London. Millicent's visits to London to see her sisters Elizabeth and Louise brought her into contact with radical groups and she met, and was influenced by, John Stuart Mill. He introduced Millicent to people campaigning for women's rights. Among these was Henry Fawcett, the blind MP for Brighton and Professor of Economics at Cambridge University, whom Millicent married in 1867. After her marriage, Millicent:

- acted as her husband's political secretary until his death in 1884;
- worked on the first Women's Suffrage Committee from 1867;
- published *Political Economy for Beginners* in 1870 and, later, *Essays and Lectures on Political Subjects*;
- contributed to framing the Married Women's Property Acts;
- organised lectures in Cambridge that led to the founding of a woman's college, Newnham, in 1871;
- supported Josephine Butler's campaign against prostitution (see page 27);
- formed a non-party suffrage society with Lydia Becker (see page 52);
- supported Clementina Black (see page 161) in her attempts to persuade the government to protect low-paid women workers;
- was President of the National Union of Women's Suffrage Societies (1897–1919) where she opposed the methods of Emmeline Pankhurst's militant campaign but not her ultimate objective;
- after the First World War, wrote *The Women's Victory* (1920), *What I Remember* (1924) and *Josephine Butler* (1927).

What were the arguments against giving votes to women?

Again, it would be best to let the people speak for themselves.

Source G

The Queen is most anxious to enlist everyone who can speak or write to join in checking this mad wicked folly of 'Women's Rights', with all its attendant horrors, on which her poor sex is bent, forgetting every sense of womanly feeling and propriety – God created men and women different – than let them remain each in their own position. Woman would become the most hateful, heartless and disgusting of human beings were she allowed to unsex herself; and where would be the protection which man was intended to give to the weaker sex?

In 1870 Theodore Martin was writing a biography of Queen Victoria's late husband, Prince Albert. This is part of a letter he received from Queen Victoria's secretary, written on her behalf. In 1908 it was printed as a pamphlet by the Men's League for Opposing Women's Suffrage.

Question

Are you surprised that the most powerful woman in the world should have been so opposed to women's suffrage?

Source H

We, the undersigned, wish to appeal to the common sense and the educated thought of the men and women of England against the proposed extension of the parliamentary suffrage to women.

Whilst desiring the fullest possible development of their powers, energies, and education of women, we believe that their work for the state, and their responsibilities towards it, must always differ essentially from those of men, and that therefore their share in the working of the State machinery should be different from that assigned to men.

To men belong the struggle of debate and legislation in parliament; the hard and exhausting labour implied in the administration of the national resources and powers; the conduct of England's relations towards the external world; the working of the army and the navy. In all these spheres, women's direct participation is made impossible either by the disabilities of sex*, or by strong formations of custom and habit resting ultimately upon physical difference, against which it is useless to contend.

In conclusion: nothing can be further from our minds than to seem to deprecate the position or the importance of women. It is because we are keenly alive to the enormous value of the special contribution to the community, that we oppose what seems to us likely to endanger that contribution. We are convinced that the pursuit of a mere outward equality with men is for women not only vain but leads to a total misconception of women's true dignity and special mission.

Signed: Dowager Lady Stanley of Alderley, Lady Frederick Cavendish, Beatrice Potter, Lady Randolph Churchill + 100 others

An 'Appeal against Female Suffrage' published in *The Nineteenth Century* (a magazine) in June 1889 and signed by over one hundred women, mostly titled

* disabilities of sex = a polite way of referring to menstruation

Source I

A permanent and vast difference of type has been impressed upon women and men respectively by the Maker of both*. Their differences of social office** rest mainly upon causes, not flexible and elastic like most mental qualities, but physical and in their nature interchangeable. I for one am not prepared to say which of the two sexes has the higher and which the lower province. But, I recognise the subtle and profound character of the differences between them.

I am not without the fear lest, beginning with the state, we should eventually be found to have intruded into what is yet more fundamental and more sacred, the precinct of the family, and should dislocate. Or injuriously modify the relations of domestic life. As this is not a party question or a class question, so neither is it a sex question. I have no fear lest the woman should encroach upon the power of the man. The fear I have is lest we should invite her unwittingly to trespass upon the delicacy, the purity, the refinement, the elevation of her own nature which are the present sources of its power.

My disposition is to take no step in advance until I am convinced of its safety.

Part of a letter written by W.E. Gladstone to Samuel Smith in 1892. Gladstone was Prime Minister and leader of the Liberal Party; Smith was a Liberal Party MP.

* i.e. God
** the philosophy of 'separate spheres'

SKILLS BUILDER

- What different reasons are suggested in Sources H and I for not giving women the vote?
- How far does Gladstone's reasoning follow that of the 'separate spheres' philosophy? (Look back at Unit 1 to remind yourself what this was about.)

Source J

Although the arguments used by those who supported and those who opposed women's suffrage largely differed, there were some surprising similarities. Firstly, most of those involved in the suffrage debate seemed to believe that votes for women was the means to an end. The suffragists, suffragettes* and the Antis** all held that the vote would bring about a social revolution, but whereas the former welcomed such change, it struck fear into the opposition. Suffragists and suffragettes looked forward to the day when women would be able to end the perceived exploitation of their sex by instituting legal changes and increasing educational and employment opportunities. For them, the vote would herald a new dawn of equality. In contrast, the Antis feared the reforming zeal of enfranchised women because it would undermine the authority of the male. One late 19th century MP maintained that a parliament elected by women would 'have more class cries, permissive legislation, domestic perplexities and sentimental grievances' and give greater importance to questions of a social nature, at the expense of constitutional and international issues.

From Paula Bartley *Votes for Women 1860–1928* published in 1998

* those who pursued female suffrage by violent, often illegal, means (see Unit 5)
** those who opposed female suffrage

How effective was the women's franchise movement 1865–1903?

How important to the cause of female suffrage was the election of John Stuart Mill to the House of Commons?

The election of John Stuart Mill to the House of Commons in 1865 was important for several reasons:

- He was elected on a female suffrage platform: although he refused to canvass, he gave a pre-election address in which he made it clear that he was in favour of giving women the vote. He agreed to Barbara Bodichon's request to present a petition to parliament in support of female suffrage.

- Barbara Bodichon (see page 22), Emily Davies, Jessie Boucherett, Elizabeth Garrett and Helen Taylor (John Stuart Mill's daughter) drew up a petition demanding the vote for all householders, regardless of their gender.

- In 1866, Barbara Bodichon formed the first Women's Suffrage Committee which within a fortnight had collected over 1,500 signatures in support of the petition.

- J.S. Mill and Henry Fawcett presented the petition to parliament where J.S. Mill made a long speech in support of female suffrage that was listened to respectfully.

For the first time, the whole issue of female suffrage was firmly on the parliamentary agenda and had been treated seriously.

What was the significance, for female suffrage, of the 1867 Reform Bill?

The 1867 Reform Act extended the franchise to include householders and lodgers who had been resident for at least twelve months. In effect, most skilled artisans and tenant farmers were added to the electoral register. But what of the women, and in particular, what of women householders? It would be wrong to suggest that women were ignored. Several petitions supporting women's suffrage were presented to parliament during the debates on the bill. Indeed, on 20 May 1867, John Stuart Mill proposed an **amendment** that the word 'person' should be substituted for the word 'man' in the bill. In this way, suitably qualified women would be entitled to vote on the same terms as men. The amendment was defeated by 196 votes to 73, but nevertheless, the subject of female enfranchisement had again been debated.

Lily Maxwell – the unexpected voter?

In January 1868, the *Englishwoman's Review*, a magazine that dealt with women's concerns, reported an exciting happening in Manchester.

Definition

Amendment

An amendment to a parliamentary bill is a change that an MP, or group of MPs, would like to make to the bill. Then, as now, MPs vote on the amendments before they vote on the actual bill.

Source K

The Case of Lily Maxwell

Lord Byron remarked on the suddenness of his rise to celebrity. 'I awoke one morning and found myself famous.' Much the same may now be said of a very different person, Mrs Lily Maxwell of Manchester. On 25th November there was nothing to distinguish her from the many other independent women who keep shops in that town. On 26th she recorded her vote for Mr Jacob Bright [the local Liberal MP who became the women's parliamentary spokesman] and at once assumed a humble place in the annals of our time. We are told that Mrs Lily Maxwell is an intelligent person of respectable appearance, and that she keeps a small shop for the sale of crockery ware. Her act is likely to produce considerable moral effect, perhaps even some legal effect also.

The Times suggests that her name was put on the register by a deep-laid plot of the Women's Suffrage Society. This was certainly not the case; for neither the Secretary of the Manchester Women's Suffrage Society, nor Mrs Maxwell herself, was aware, until a day or two before the election, that her name was on the register of electors. When informed of the circumstance, Lily Maxwell at once announced her readiness to vote. It is sometimes said that women, especially those of the working class, have no political opinion at all, and would not care to vote. Yet this woman, who by chance was furnished with a vote, professed strong political opinions, and was delighted to have a chance of expressing them.

Accordingly, on the following day she went to Mr Bright's committee-room, accompanied by Miss Becker, the able and zealous secretary of the Manchester Suffrage Society, and by another lady, also a member of the Committee. From thence the ladies were escorted by several gentlemen to the polling-place, which was a large room containing several booths. Mrs Maxwell's name being on the list of electors, the returning officer had no choice in the matter, but was bound to accept her vote.

As soon as it was given, the other voters in the room, whether supporters of Mr Bright's or of the other candidates, united in three hearty cheers for the heroine of the day.

SKILLS BUILDER

- What evidence is there in this source that the author was in favour of female suffrage?
- What evidence is there in this source that not everyone approved of what Lily Maxwell did?

Was Lily the only one?

No, she was not! Lydia Becker got to work and discovered that other women had been included, in error, on electoral registers. In Manchester, thirteen women were entered on electoral registers and nine of them voted in the 1868 general election. Over 5,000 women householders in Manchester promptly applied to be added to the registers. The situation seemed to some to be getting out of hand. Was this female enfranchisement by the back door?

Clearly something had to be done. Could women householders be included on electoral registers, or not? A test case, Chorlton v Lings, was held in the

High Court in 1868. Lawyers on the women's side, among them Richard Pankhurst (see pages 43 and 80) argued that women had the right to vote under ancient English law. But they lost because the judge decided that English custom overruled this.

Trying, trying and trying again

In 1870, Richard Pankhurst tried again and drafted the first Women's Suffrage Bill. It was introduced into the House of Commons as a Private Members' Bill and passed its first and second readings. However, when the Liberal Prime Minister W.E. Gladstone made it clear that the government would not support such a bill, it was finally defeated. But the pressure was on. Women's suffrage bills were introduced regularly throughout the 1870s and, on the few occasions they gained a majority of votes in the Commons, the government made sure they did not pass into law.

Throughout the 1870s, the early suffragists focused on petitioning, lobbying MPs and producing pamphlets arguing their cause. Their lack of success, however, led to friction.

Biography

Lydia Becker 1827–90

Lydia Becker was born in Manchester, the eldest of fifteen children. Her father Hannibal owned a successful chemical works. Lydia was educated at home and, when her mother died in 1855, supervised the upbringing of her younger brothers and sisters. She was a keen member of the Manchester Ladies' Literary Society. Lydia was interested in botany; in 1864 she won an award for her collection of dried plants and two years later published *Botany for Novices*. She was so good a botanist that she and Charles Darwin corresponded with each other. Everything changed, however, when in 1866 she attended a lecture in Manchester given by Barbara Bodichon about women's suffrage. From that point on, Lydia:

- wrote an article 'Female Suffrage' that was published in the magazine *Contemporary Review*;
- worked with Emily Davis and Elizabeth Wolstenholme Elmy to form the Manchester Women's Suffrage Committee in 1867 and became its secretary;
- became treasurer of the Married Women's Property Committee in 1868;
- founded the *Women's Suffrage Journal* in 1870 and became its editor throughout the 1870s and 1880s;
- worked with Josephine Butler in her campaign against the Contagious Diseases Acts;
- was elected to the Manchester School Board in 1870 and took a particular interest in the education of girls, suggesting, among other things, that girls should be taught less domestic science and that boys should be taught to cook;
- created outrage in the women's suffrage movement by supporting the idea that the vote should be given, first, to single women; opposed in this by married women suffragists, she was forced to resign from the Married Women's Committee in 1874.

Becoming ill in 1890, Lydia was advised to visit the health spa of Aix-les-Bains, where she caught diphtheria and died.

Disagreements, disputes and divisions

The Women's Suffrage Committee, formed in London in 1866 was mirrored by the founding, in the same year, of the Manchester National Society for Women's Suffrage, with Lydia Becker as its secretary. Rapidly, similar organisations were founded in Birmingham, Bristol and Edinburgh as well as in Ireland. But there was trouble ahead. Like almost all single-issue groups, the goal was clear but there were strong arguments about strategy and tactics causing the various different groups to split and re-form.

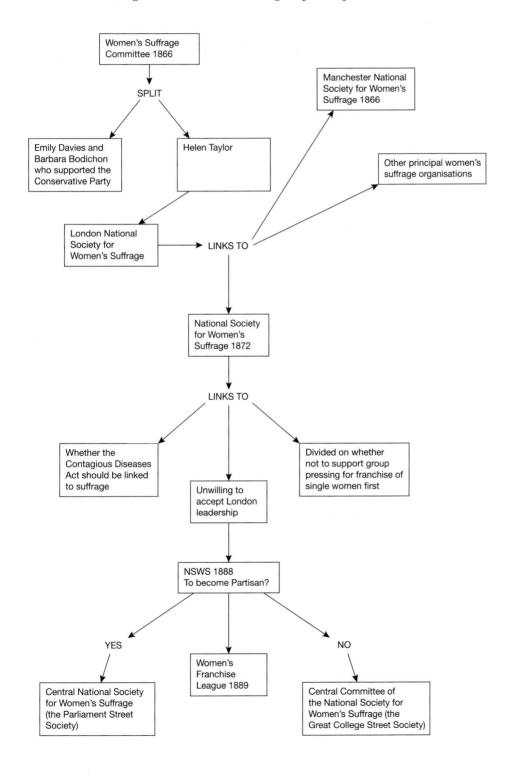

How damaging were the disputes and divisions to the cause of female suffrage?

Disputes and divisions usually weaken a movement. However, read what the historian in Source L has to say.

> ## Source L
>
> Wherever a Women's Liberal Association existed which was affiliated to the 'new' Central Committee, there were in effect two women's suffrage associations, but nowhere do there appear to have been two organisations actually calling themselves specifically suffrage societies. This points to a basic unity of purpose in the movement. The desire behind many suffragists to avoid public disagreement was probably behind the decision of societies such as Birmingham to remain separate from either of the two central organisations.
>
> From R. Billington 'Women, Politics and Local Liberalism: From "Female Suffrage" to "Votes for Women"' in *Journal for Regional and Local Studies* vol. 5 published in 1985

Indeed, the Parliament Street Society and the Great College Street Society worked together in the run up to the 1894 Local Government Act. This important Act gave married women the same rights as single women to vote in local elections, sit on school boards and work as guardians of the poor. At a stroke, the main source of division between the two main suffrage societies was removed. The way lay open to amalgamation and one single suffrage society.

The National Union of Women's Suffrage Societies

Inspired by the 1894 Local Government Act, a conference for delegates from all the female suffrage groups was held in Birmingham two years later, with the aim of formulating a petition to parliament asking for women's suffrage. The petition, containing some 250,000 signatures, was presented to parliament in 1897 in support of the Women's Suffrage Bill, proposed by a Conservative MP, Faithful Begg. The bill passed its second reading with a 71-vote majority (230 to 159) and then, like all Private Members' Bills before it, failed to become law because of government opposition. This was an important turning point in parliamentary support: the first of a series of **parliamentary divisions** in favour of women's suffrage.

In Source M, historian Ray Strachey explains the impact this had on the women's suffrage societies.

It was from this point onwards that the NUWSS co-ordinated the constitutional campaign for women's suffrage and continued to do so until 1918. Millicent Fawcett continued to insist on a non-party approach, urging women to work for whichever MP or prospective MP supported female suffrage, and refusing to work for those who would not.

Definition

Parliamentary divisions

Members of parliament register their votes on specific bills, debates and in committees by dividing. The results of the vote are referred to as Divisions. The Division List records how MPs have voted. The same process happens in the House of Lords.

Source M

The societies, which had already been moving towards reunion, now took the matter up in real earnest. The two London societies became one central society and, with the eighteen provincial ones, grouped themselves in a national organisation of which Mrs [Millicent] Fawcett was the President, and adopted a regular, democratic constitution under the name of the National Union of Women's Suffrage Societies.

From Ray Strachey The Cause: A Short History of the Women's Movement in Great Britain published in 1928

Source N

Constitutional suffragists like these considered the vote as evidence that they were winning, and that reform would come if they continued to use their current methods. But since gaining a parliamentary majority had not led to suffrage legislation, others saw it as proof that the use of moderate methods had failed. This encouraged some to explore militant methods in an attempt to force the government to enact women's suffrage.

From Harold L. Smith The British Women's Suffrage Campaign 1866–1928 published in 1998

But there were problems, as Source N suggests.

This 'exploration of militant methods' will be considered in the next unit.

Unit summary

What have you learned in this unit?

By 1903 the question of women's suffrage had been debated several times in parliament and there was growing support in the House of Commons for giving women the vote. However, the bills presented had been Private Members' Bills and, because they had not had government backing, did not succeed in becoming law. Many different organisations in support of female enfranchisement had grown and developed throughout the country. In 1897 the majority of these organisations and groups came together in the National Union of Women's Suffrage Societies under the presidency of Millicent Fawcett. They were dedicated to achieving votes for women by legal means: by persuasion through argument, letters, pamphlets, public meetings, marches and demonstrations. However, by 1903 some suffragists were becoming restless and beginning to demand more forceful and confrontational methods.

What skills have you used in this unit?

You will have understood that progress to a specific goal does not happen steadily and that evaluation of source material can lead to an understanding of why progress may seem to be advancing well and at other times, stalled. You will have kept in mind the work you have done on the earlier units regarding the prevailing attitudes to women and the efforts made by women themselves to bring about change to their perceived role.

SKILLS BUILDER

1 Study Sources A–E. In what ways has the argument for giving women the vote developed and changed between 1866 and 1907? Can you think of reasons for this? (You'll need to look back over Units 2 and 3 and think of significant milestones including such things as legislation.)

2 Set up a debate 'This House believes women should not be given the vote.' Remember to use arguments from the time (for and against) when you make out your case.

3 Back to the start: How effective was the women's franchise movement in the years to 1903?

Exam tips

This is the sort of question you will find appearing on the examination paper as a (b) question.

4 Read Sources F, I and J and use your own knowledge.

Do you agree with the view, expressed in Source J, that there were surprising similarities between the arguments of those who supported, and those who opposed women's suffrage?

You tackled a (b) style question at the end of Unit 2. Look back at the Exam tips you were given there (see page 29). Now is the time to build on and develop those tips. What do you have to do to write a successful answer to a (b) question?

- What is the **view** being expressed in Source J? Read Source J carefully and write the 'view' in the middle of what will be a spider diagram.
- Read Sources F and I carefully. Establish points that **support** and **challenge** the view and set those as spider 'legs'.
- **Think** about appropriate **knowledge** and add a note of this to the different spider 'legs', using knowledge to both **reinforce** and **challenge**.
- **Cross-reference** between the different 'legs' for **similarities** and **differences**.

You are now ready to write up your answer.

Remember to:

- combine the different points into arguments for and against the stated view;
- evaluate the conflicting arguments by reference to the quality of the evidence used;
- reach a supported judgement.

RESEARCH TASK

Charles Darwin

You read that Lydia Becker was such a good botanist that she corresponded with Charles Darwin.

- Who was Charles Darwin?

- What was his greatest achievement?

- How could this achievement be used (a) to challenge and (b) to support the theory of 'separate spheres'?

5 Adding militancy to the campaign 1903–14

What is this unit about?

This unit focuses on the increasing militancy of the campaign for women's suffrage and on the ways in which this militancy was expressed. In this unit you will:

- find out why some women decided to adopt a militant approach;
- discover how the addition of militancy changed the nature of the campaign;
- evaluate source material in order to develop an understanding of the nature of the **militant** campaign.

Key questions

- In what ways did the campaign for women's suffrage become militant?
- How did the Pankhursts organise the Women's Social and Political Union (WSPU) so that it could deliver militancy?

Historical health warning!

This unit, and the one that follows it, cover roughly the same time period, but in different ways. This unit focuses on the twentieth-century militant campaign for the enfranchisement of women; the next unit addresses the reactions of individuals and groups to that campaign. They have been separated out for reasons of clarity, but you will need to cross-reference between the two units in order to gain the fullest understanding of the dynamics of the period.

> **Definition**
>
> **Militant**
>
> Aggressively active in pursuing a social or political end. Militancy means being involved in militant activities.

Timeline

1903	Women's Social and Political Union founded by Emmeline Pankhurst
1905	Christabel Pankhurst and Annie Kenney arrested for causing a disturbance
1906	WSPU moved to London
	Daily Mail nicknames WSPU members 'suffragettes'
1907	*Votes for Women* founded
	Charlotte Despard and Teresa Billington-Grieg expelled from WSPU
1908	Women chained themselves to railings for the first time
	Beginning of organised heckling of Cabinet ministers
	'Women's Sunday' organised by WSPU
	First window smashing
1910	'Black Friday'
1911	*March of the Women* composed by Ethel Smyth

1912	Emmeline and Frederick Pethick-Lawrence leave the WSPU
	Emmeline Pankhurst makes speech urging greater militancy
1913	Emily Davison dies at the Epsom Derby
1914	Sylvia Pankhurst expelled from the WSPU

Source A

Shout, shout – up with your song,
Cry with the wind for the dawn is breaking;
March, march, swing you along,
Wide blows our banner, and hope is waking.
Song with its story, dreams with their glory.
Lo! they call, and glad is their word!
Hark, hark, hear how it swells,
Thunder of freedom, the voice of the Lord!

Life, strife – these two are one.
Naught can you win but by faith and daring.
On, on – that ye have done
But for the work of today preparing.
Firm in reliance, laugh a defiance –
(Laugh in hope, for sure is the end)
March, march, many as one,
Shoulder to shoulder and friend to friend.

The first and last verses of a song *The March of the Women*
composed by Ethel Smyth in 1911

Question

On what kind of occasions would you imagine this song would be sung? And by whom?

SKILLS BUILDER

What is this song suggesting about the women's suffrage campaign? Can you detect a change from the campaigning you read about in Unit 4?

Why did the Pankhursts begin their militant campaign?

A lot of the sources you will read in this unit come from the writings of various members of the Pankhurst family themselves. Beware! They were a volatile family, given to arguing, splitting up and making and breaking friendships. Their writings, therefore, are not necessarily objective. As a family, their activities within the women's suffrage movement have given rise both to criticism and praise, at the time and from historians afterwards.

Beginning the campaign

Emmeline Pankhurst seems to have developed the idea of forming a new organisation after the death of her husband, Richard, in 1898. Forced to take paid work in order to support their four children, she became a registrar of births and deaths in Manchester.

Source B

In this work, she met many despairing working class women, burdened with over-numerous families; in particular, she was especially moved by the plight of single mothers, some of them as young as 13, who, having been seduced by a father or close male relative, came to register the birth of their babies. Her conviction grew that, if women were to progress, they had to lift themselves out of their subordinate position and campaign for the parliamentary vote.

From J. Purvis 'Emmeline Pankhurst (1858–1928) and Votes for Women'
in J. Purvis and S. Holton *Votes for Women* published in 2000

A radical newspaper began a fund to support Emmeline and her family. Emmeline, however, refused the cash and insisted instead that it was used to build a socialist meeting hall. Both Emmeline and Richard had been active members of the newly formed ILP and so this seemed entirely appropriate. However, Emmeline was horrified to find that the ILP branch that was intending to use the newly built hall was not allowing women to be members. She turned to forming her own organisation.

Source C

It was in October 1903 that I invited a number of women to my house in Nelson Street, Manchester, for the purposes of organisation. We voted to call the new society the Women's Social and Political Union, partly to emphasise its democracy and partly to identify its object as political rather than propagandist. We resolved to limit our membership exclusively to women, to keep ourselves absolutely free from any party affiliation, to be satisfied with nothing but action on our question. Deeds, not words, was to be our permanent motto.

From Emmeline Pankhurst *My Own Story* published in 1914

SKILLS BUILDER

- Prioritise the reasons you can find so far in Sources B, C and the text for the formation of yet another organisation arguing for women to be given the vote; share this with other students in your group. To what extent do you agree?
- Is there anything, yet, to make you think that this organisation would be likely to be any different from the NUWSS?

Becoming militant

It is important to understand what being 'militant' meant at the time. In the 1860s, when this book begins, it would have been considered 'militant' to have attended, or to have dared to speak, at a public meeting; by the early twentieth century it would be 'militant' to have heckled ministers and MPs and to have carried banners; by 1912, militancy was associated with window smashing and arson.

If 'deeds, not words', was to be the WSPU's motto, then there has to be some sort of explanation as to why Emmeline and her followers did not consider the NUWSS an appropriate organisation to support. The NUWSS, after all, wrote pamphlets, lobbied MPs and held meetings, which were all deeds. The next source gives a clear indication of what, initially, the WSPU meant by 'deeds, not words'.

Source D

Good seats were secured for the Free Trade Hall meeting. The question was painted on a banner in large letters, in case it should not be made clear enough by vocal utterance. How should we word it? 'Will you give women suffrage?' We rejected that form – "Let them suffer away!" – we had heard the taunt. We must find another wording – and we did! It was so obvious and yet, strange to say, quite new. Our banner bore this terse device:

WILL YOU GIVE

VOTES

FOR WOMEN?

Thus was uttered for the first time the famous and victorious battle-cry 'Votes for Women!'

Busy with white calico, black furniture stain and paint-brushes, we soon had our banner ready, and Annie Kenney and I set forth to victory, in the form of an affirmative Liberal answer, or to prison.

The Free Trade Hall was crowded. The sky was clear for a Liberal victory – save for a little cloud no bigger than a woman's hand! Calm, but with beating hearts, Annie and I took our seats and looked at the exultant throng we must soon anger by our challenge. Their cheers as the speakers entered gave us the note and pitch of their emotion. Speech followed speech. Our plan was to wait until the speakers had said their say, before asking our question. We must, for one thing, give these Liberal leaders and spokesmen the opportunity of explaining that their programme included political enfranchisement for women.

Annie as the working woman – for this should make the stronger appeal to Liberals – rose first and asked 'Will the Liberal government give votes to women?' No answer came. I joined my voice to hers and our banner was unfurled, making clear what was our question. The effect was explosive! The meeting was aflame with excitement!

From Christabel Pankhurst *Unshackled: The Story of How We Won the Vote* published in 1959. Here she is describing a meeting in the Free Trade Hall, Manchester, in October 1905.

Aflame with excitement it may have been, but **Annie Kenney** (see page 80) and **Christabel Pankhurst** (see page 80) were arrested and charged with assaulting the police and with causing an obstruction in South Street. Christabel had spat at a police officer and struck him across the face with her gloves, and, after being ejected from the meeting, she and Annie Kenney tried to hold an impromptu meeting outside to explain their views. Refusing to pay the fines imposed by the magistrates, Annie and Christabel were imprisoned in Strangeways gaol, Annie for three days and Christabel for seven.

Source E

We rose at four o'clock on a dark October morning to take the journey from Ashton-under-Lyne to Strangeways prison, to greet Christabel on her release. When we arrived at the prison gates, we found a large crowd had assembled, among whom I remember were members of the Women's Trade Union Council, Eva Gore-Booth, and other members of the older suffrage societies, and a large contingent of the Manchester ILP.

Twenty years of peaceful propaganda had not produced such an effect, nor had fifty years of patient pleading which had gone before. The smouldering resentment in women's hearts burst into a flame of revolt. There began one of the strangest battles in all our English history. It was fitting, indeed, that it began on the site of Peterloo, where three-quarters of a century before, a vast crowd of men and women met to demand the franchise, only to be trampled down by the Yeomanry sent out to disperse them.

The North was roused, and neither Sir Edward Grey nor his party were ever able to damp down the fire they lit on that October evening in 1905.

> From Hannah Mitchell's autobiography *The Hard Way Up* published in 1977. Born into a poor family in the Derbyshire Peak District, Hannah ran away from home, finding work as a domestic servant and in a number of sweatshops. Living in the Manchester area after her marriage in 1895, she and her husband Gibbon were drawn into the Labour movement and, in 1903 Hannah joined the WSPU.

SKILLS BUILDER

- Can we trust Source D to be giving an accurate account of the meeting in the Free Trade Hall in Manchester in October 1905?
- What can be learned from Sources D and E about the nature of the WSPU and its supporters?

Source F

With one accord, the brawling and wickedness of the women were deplored [in the Press] and the leader-writers lamented with sham regret that their cause was put back for ages and that women had now proved themselves forever unfit for enfranchisement. Manchester University (where Christabel had already been troublesome by insisting on being a law student) threatened to expel her, and the whole affair was the great pre-occupation of the city. Already, by this one act, hundreds of people who had never thought about women's suffrage before, began to consider it and, though the vast majority of them deplored what had been done, this did not make the result any the less important. A wonderful new weapon, the weapon of publicity and advertisement, was put in the hands of the Women's Social and Political Union and the leaders at once saw its value.

From Ray Strachey *The Cause: A Short History of the Women's Movement in Great Britain* published in 1928. Here she is commenting on events in Manchester in October 1905. She was a member of the NUWSS.

Source G

Over the years non-militant methods had failed and attempts to promote backbench bills seemed futile. Instead, women should attack the government of the day until it agreed to introduce its own legislation for women's suffrage. A militant campaign would push suffrage up the agenda and, by rousing the country, force the Cabinet to back down.

From Martin Pugh *Votes for Women in Britain 1867–1928* published in 1994

SKILLS BUILDER

How far do Sources F and G agree about the importance of mounting a militant campaign?

In January 1906 the *Daily Mail*, critical of the WSPU, called its members 'suffragettes'. The name stuck. From then onwards, the fight for female suffrage was conducted mainly by the NUWSS led by **Millicent Fawcett** (see page 47) and the WSPU led by Emmeline Pankhurst.

How was the WSPU organised?

The WSPU, from 1906 onwards, was a strongly hierarchical organisation, as can be seen from the following diagram.

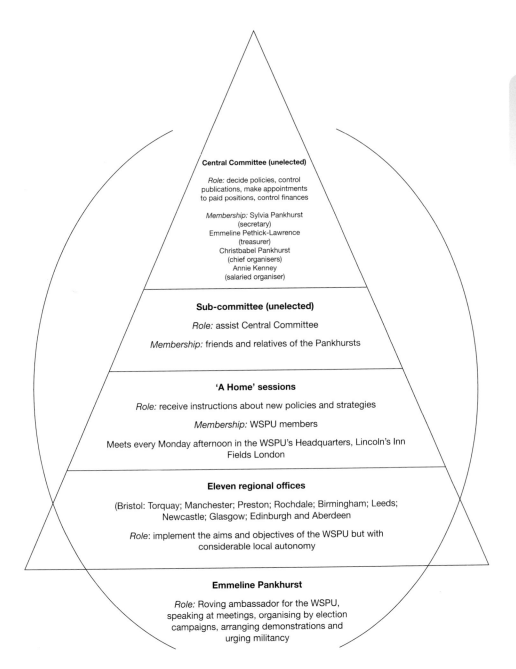

Central Committee (unelected)

Role: decide policies, control publications, make appointments to paid positions, control finances

Membership: Sylvia Pankhurst (secretary)
Emmeline Pethick-Lawrence (treasurer)
Christbabel Pankhurst (chief organisers)
Annie Kenney (salaried organiser)

Sub-committee (unelected)

Role: assist Central Committee

Membership: friends and relatives of the Pankhursts

'A Home' sessions

Role: receive instructions about new policies and strategies

Membership: WSPU members

Meets every Monday afternoon in the WSPU's Headquarters, Lincoln's Inn Fields London

Eleven regional offices

(Bristol: Torquay; Manchester; Preston; Rochdale; Birmingham; Leeds; Newcastle; Glasgow; Edinburgh and Aberdeen

Role: implement the aims and objectives of the WSPU but with considerable local autonomy

Emmeline Pankhurst

Role: Roving ambassador for the WSPU, speaking at meetings, organising by election campaigns, arranging demonstrations and urging militancy

Question

What would be the strengths, and what would be the weaknesses, of a structure like this?

Why was this way of organising the WSPU criticised so much?

This autocratic structure was criticised at the time and has been criticised by historians since.

- It was considered hypocritical of the WSPU to demand greater democracy from a Liberal government while not being prepared to exercise it within their own organisation.

- It was thought that votes for women should be sought through an organisation that mirrored the British constitutional set-up, which clearly the WSPU did not.

- It was felt inappropriate to seek for female enfranchisement through an organisation run solely by women when the world of politics with which enfranchised women would have to deal was a world that contained both men and women.

But there are, of course, counter arguments:

- Emmeline Pankhurst never claimed that the WSPU was democratic: she simply considered the structure she devised to be the most effective way of achieving its goals.
- Branches outside London had complete flexibility to be as democratic as they wished.
- A democratically organised structure would never work once the activities of the WSPU became illegal, and this was what Emmeline and Christabel argued.
- Although it may not have been democratic, the leadership went to great lengths to involve the membership and many suffragettes spoke warmly of the training they had in public speaking and the confidence this gave them to defend their aims and objectives.

Question

How appropriate was the structure of the WSPU?

Disputes and expulsions

WSPU members could, of course, always resign if they didn't like the way the organisation was run or if they didn't like the way it was developing. But what seemed to happen in the WSPU was that Emmeline and Christabel Pankhurst expelled those members with whom they disagreed. There were many arguments and disagreements between 1903 and 1914, but the following three were the main ones.

Dispute 1, Summer 1907

Charlotte Despard and Teresa Billington-Grieg, disturbed by the WSPU's cultivation of middle- and upper-class women with money, and anxious that the WSPU should not lose touch with the working class, drew up a written constitution. They wanted greater autonomy for the regional branches, elected leaders and greater involvement of members in policy decisions. Unsurprisingly, at the WSPU conference, Emmeline Pankhurst, in a melodramatic scene, denounced Charlotte and Teresa as traitors, tore up the constitution and announced to the delegates that she was the Commander-in-Chief of an army in which they were the foot-soldiers. As a direct result, Charlotte Despard, Teresa Billington-Grieg and about one fifth of the WSPU membership left and formed the Women's Freedom League. 'If we are fighting against the subjection of woman to man', declared Teresa, 'we cannot honestly submit to the subjection of woman to woman.'

Definition

Non-partisan

Not committed to any side.

Interestingly, the WFL was not itself to be free from internal divisions and disputes. It supported militancy and illegal actions but from a democratic base and, although supposedly **non-partisan**, worked with local Labour groups and supported Labour candidates at elections and by-elections.

Dispute 2, October 1912

The Pankhursts could be equally ruthless with their friends. Emmeline and Frederick Pethick-Lawrence were close friends of the Pankhursts. Indeed, the Pethick-Lawrences had been founder members of the WSPU and Christabel had lived with them when she moved to London in 1906. However, the Pethick-Lawrences began to question the escalation of violence (see pages 57–80) and, with the added embarrassment of Frederick being of the 'wrong' gender, they were summarily expelled from the WSPU. Remarkably, they seemed to bear the Pankhursts no ill-will and continued to edit the WSPU journal *Votes for Women*. Two years after their expulsion from the WSPU, Emmeline and Frederick Pethick-Lawrence founded the United Suffragists that was closely linked to the left-wing of the Labour movement.

Dispute 3, January 1914

Ruthlessness with colleagues and friends was nothing compared to ruthlessness within the Pankhurst family. Sylvia Pankhurst ran the East London Federation of Suffragettes (ELFS), a branch of the WSPU that focused on achieving a range of rights and benefits for working-class women, and was certainly democratic in organisation. Summoned by her sister and told to focus her activities on one goal and to disassociate the ELFS from the Labour movement, Sylvia refused to back down. The ELFS was summarily removed as a branch of the WSPU and, cut off from its funds, was never really able to operate as a force in the suffrage movement. However, Sylvia continued to edit her own paper the *Women's Dreadnought* and continued her work among working-class women in the east end of London.

Did the WSPU ignore working-class women?

It is clear that Sylvia Pankhurst was very involved with the problems, rights and opportunities of working-class women in the east end of London. Historians, however, disagree about whether or not the WSPU as an organisation was interested in the plight of working-class women.

> **Question**
>
> In your judgement, did these expulsions help or harm the WSPU? Use this as a discussion point in your group.

> **Question**
>
> How is it possible for historians to hold such different views?

Source H

The WSPU was set up specifically for working class women and, between 1903 and 1906, did valuable propaganda work in the textile towns. Even when the WSPU headquarters moved to London, it targeted working class women. When Annie Kenney, a cotton worker recruited at a WSPU meeting in Oldham, and Sylvia Pankhurst were sent to London to organise the campaign in the capital, most of their energies were spent in working class districts. Moreover, the first London branch of the WSPU was formed at Canning Town in the East End.

From Paula Bartley *Votes for Women 1860–1928* published in 1998

Source I

After their move to London in 1906, the Pankhursts abandoned any attempt to mobilise the Lancashire cotton textile girls. However, they took care to retain one, Annie Kenney, whose function was to prove that working class women wanted the vote. The Pankhursts threw their energies into cultivating the Conservative leaders and tapping the funds and support of metropolitan society.

From Martin Pugh *The Tories and the People 1880–1935* published in 1985

How well supported were the campaigns for women's suffrage?

The NUWSS and the WSPU dominated the campaign for women's suffrage, and it is tempting to see them as two entirely separate organisations, organising separate campaigns, frequently at loggerheads with each other and attracting very different sorts of people as members. The truth is far more complex. Many women joined both organisations; the NUWSS and WSPU held joint meetings and demonstrations; and members of the NUWSS held celebratory dinners for WSPU suffragettes released from prison. The situation is further complicated by the fact that, whilst the NUWSS published membership figures, the WSPU did not.

Membership of both organisations increased dramatically after about 1909, as historian Martin Pugh explains in Source J.

Source J

From 1909 onwards, militancy appears to have had an important indirect effect on the membership of the NUWSS, which rose from 12,000 to over 50,000. The explanation is that many women who had no wish to be associated with the suffragettes could not help being moved by their example and, therefore, chose to express their feelings by joining the non-militants.

From Martin Pugh *Votes for Women in Britain 1867–1928*
published in 1994

Historian Brian Harrison agrees, and provides more detail about the NUWSS in Source K.

Source K

The non-militants remained organisationally, numerically and educationally superior throughout the period and maintained their growth rate more successfully. The number of NUWSS branches rose from 33 in October 1907 to 70 in March 1910 and 478 in February 1914. If local and national funds are aggregated, the non-militant total had reached about £45,000 in the financial year 1913–14.

From B. Harrison *Women's Suffrage at Westminster 1866–1928*
published in 1983

Source L

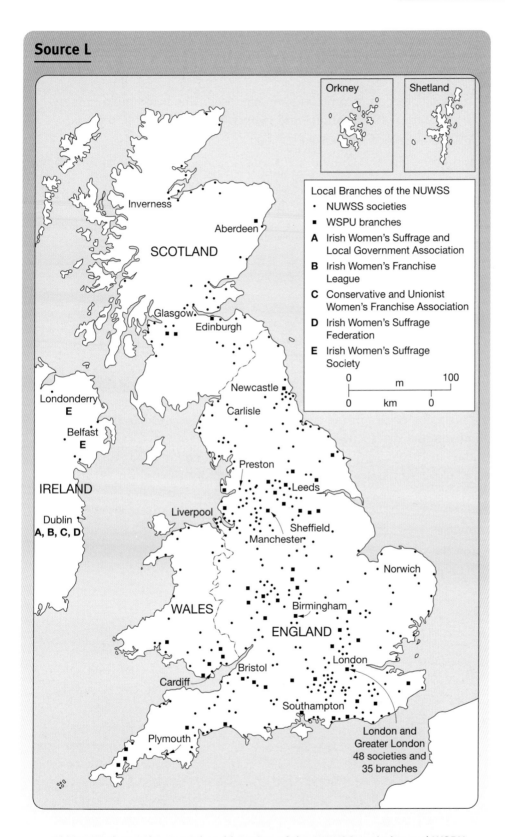

Orkney

Shetland

Local Branches of the NUWSS
- · NUWSS societies
- ▪ WSPU branches
- **A** Irish Women's Suffrage and Local Government Association
- **B** Irish Women's Franchise League
- **C** Conservative and Unionist Women's Franchise Association
- **D** Irish Women's Suffrage Federation
- **E** Irish Women's Suffrage Society

0   m   100
0   km   0

Inverness

Aberdeen

SCOTLAND

Glasgow

Edinburgh

Londonderry
E

Newcastle

Carlisle

Belfast
E

Preston

Leeds

IRELAND

Liverpool

Sheffield

Dublin
A, B, C, D

Manchester

Norwich

WALES

Birmingham

ENGLAND

Bristol

London

Cardiff

Southampton

London and Greater London 48 societies and 35 branches

Plymouth

5.1 This map shows the spread and location of the NUWSS societies and WSPU branches in 1914. The WSPU did not spread to Ireland, although several constitutionalist societies did so.

It is much more difficult to obtain information about the WSPU. However, historians Bartley and Harrison have managed to unearth the following statistics:

- the WSPU had an income large enough to enable it to employ ninety-eight women office workers and twenty-six officers in the regions;
- in 1913–14, the WSPU raised £37,000;
- at their height, the London 'At Home' sessions were attended by around 1,000 people per week;
- the circulation of *Votes for Women*, the WSPU newspaper, reached 30,000–40,000 per issue.

SKILLS BUILDER

What conclusions can you draw about the relative strengths of the NUWSS and the WSPU?

Three enquiries

You are now going to work through something a bit different: three enquiries that are based solely on sources. The first is a breadth enquiry that addresses the changing nature of the campaign for women's suffrage; the second is a depth enquiry that focuses on the violence meted out to suffragettes on 'Black Friday' in 1910; and the third is another depth enquiry that considers the significance of the death of the suffragette Emily Davison in 1913.

Enquiry one: To what extent did the militant campaign for votes for women change in the years to 1914?

Study the sources that follow and then answer the questions at the end of this enquiry.

Enquiry source 1A

GREAT VOTES FOR WOMEN DEMONSTRATION IN HYDE PARK, SUNDAY. JUNE 21. 1908.

5.2 A photograph taken of 'Women's Sunday' held in Hyde Park on Sunday 21 June 1908. WSPU branches from all over the country converged on Hyde Park with their banners demanding votes for women. At least eight platforms were erected around the Park on which various speakers addressed the rally. It was estimated that some 300,000 people attended.

Enquiry source 1B

5.3 A photograph of Una Dugdale canvassing in the Newcastle by-election held in September 1908. Una accompanied Emmeline Pankhurst on both of her Scottish tours. In 1912 Una married Victor Duval, the founder of the Men's Political Union for Women's Enfranchisement. She caused quite a lot of excitement when she refused to repeat the word 'obey' in her marriage vows. Both Una's sisters, Joan and Daisy, were suffragettes as well.

Enquiry source 1C

The shop itself is a blaze of purple, white and green [the suffragette colours]. Just now the Women's Press is showing some beautiful motor and other scarves in various shades of purple as well as white muslin summer blouses, and among the almost unending variety of bags, belts etc are the noticeable 'The Emmeline', and 'Christabel' bags and 'The Pethick' tobacco pouch. In addition to books, pamphlets and leaflets, stationery, games, blotters, playing cards and indeed almost everything that can be produced in purple, white or green, or a combination of all three is to be found here.

> From *Votes for Women* the suffragette journal, published in July 1910. Here the writer is describing the range of goods for sale in The Woman's Press shop, 156 Charing Cross Road, London, that was opened in May 1910.

Enquiry source 1D

What do we mean when we say we are going to continue the militant agitation for women's suffrage? There is something that governments care for far more than they care for human life, and that is the security of property. Property to them is far dearer and tenderer than is human life, and so it is through property we shall strike the enemy. I have no quarrel with property, ladies and gentlemen, and it is only as an instrument of warfare in this revolution of ours that we make attacks upon property. I think there are a great many people who own property who understand it very well, but if they would only understand it a little more quickly they would do what we want them to do. We want them to go to the government and say, 'Examine the causes that lead to the destruction of property. Remove the discontent. Remove the sense of outrage.'

We women Suffragists have a great mission, the greatest mission the world has ever known. It is to free half the human race. You, women in this meeting, will you help us to do it? (Yes!) Well, then, if you will, put aside all craven fear. Go and buy your hammer; be militant. Be militant in your own way. Those of you who can express your militancy by going to the House of Commons and refusing to leave without satisfaction, do so. Those of you who can express their militancy by facing party mobs at Cabinet ministers meetings, do so. Those of you who can express your militancy by joining us in anti-Government by-election policy – do so. Those of you who can break windows (great applause), those of you who can still further attack the sacred idol of property so as to make the Government realise that property is as greatly endangered by women as it was by the Chartists of old days – do so. And my last word is to the Government. I incite this meeting to rebellion. You have not dared to take the leaders of Ulster for their incitement to rebellion, take me if you dare.

From 'Emmeline Pankhurst at the Albert Hall' in *The Suffragette* published in 25 October 1912. On 17 October, Emmeline Pankhurst made a speech in the Albert Hall, urging militancy upon her followers.

Enquiry source 1E

From the Town Mall Square in Portsmouth I jumped on a bike and went with a friend to the beach at Southsea and sat on the beach and filled my pockets with pebbles, the idea being that I should take those in my pockets to London and if whatever we had to use in London ran out, I would always have something to fall back on.

I was given the top of Villiers Street. To fill in time I went over and bought a bunch of violets, then I bought an evening paper, and then I looked at the clock and it was a quarter to six, and that was my moment.

In my right hand I had a hammer, my pockets of my raincoat were bulging with pebbles, and I went over to the corner shop. There were two people looking at rings, a young boy and a girl. I waited, they moved and then – bang went my hammer, and it was a great moment for me because I was so afraid that the hammer would hook, and hook me into the glass and stop me doing any more. But I found, by taking my hammer broadside, that that didn't happen at all; it came back with me and so on I went. And I walked down the Strand as though I was playing hockey, and I just boldly went on like that, and I did at least nine windows.

Charlotte (Charlie) Marsh remembers going window smashing in 1912 when she was twenty-five years old, and explains how she did it

Enquiry source 1F

5.4 A photograph of Lady White's house, burned down by suffragettes on 20 March 1913. No one was hurt in the blaze, and the suffragettes would have made sure that no people or pets were inside. Lady White was a well-known opponent of women's suffrage.

PRACTICE SOURCE EVALUATION

- List the different types of sources here. Give each source a ranking out of five for reliability as evidence of suffragette militancy, where 5 is extremely reliable as evidence and 1 is extremely unreliable.
- Take the two sources you have ranked as the least reliable and, for each one, explain why.
- Take the two sources you have ranked as the most reliable and, for each one, explain why.

Remember that source evaluation isn't an end in itself, but is a means to an end and that end is effectively to answer historical questions by using the sources as evidence to support your answer. So now use the source evaluation you have completed to help you answer this question:

To what extent do the sources show that the militant campaign for votes for women changed in the years 1908–1914?

SKILLS BUILDER

1 Study Sources 1A, 1D and 1F and use your own knowledge.

To what extent would it be true to say that Mrs Pankhurst's speech (Source 1D) marked a turning point in the WSPU's militant campaign to achieve votes for women?

2 Study Sources 1B, 1D and 1E and use your own knowledge.

Do you agree with the view that militancy achieved nothing?

(You will need to cross-refer to the next unit in order to answer this question.)

Enquiry two: What really happened on 'Black Friday', 18 November 1910?

On Friday 18 November 1910 when parliament re-assembled, Prime Minister Asquith, outlining the government's programme, failed to mention female suffrage. Anticipating this, Emmeline Pankhurst led a deputation of some 300 women, broken into small groups, to the House of Commons. What happened then has passed into suffragette history as 'Black Friday'.

Enquiry source 2A

(135 sworn statements were made by suffragettes about what happened to them that day. These are three of them.)

1 For hours one was beaten about the body, thrown backwards and forwards from one to another, until one felt dazed with the horror of it. One policeman picked me up in his arms and threw me into the crowd saying, 'You come again, you B_ B_, and I will show you what I will do to you.' A favourite trick was pinching the upper parts of one's arms, which were black and blue afterwards.

2 Several times constables and plain-clothes men who were in the crowd passed their arms round me from the back and clutched hold of my breasts in as public a manner as possible, and men in the crowd followed their example. I was also pummelled on the chest, and my breast was clutched by one constable from the front. My skirt was lifted up as high as possible, and the constable attempted to lift me off the ground by raising his knee. This he could not do, so he threw me into the crowd and incited the men to treat me as they wished. Consequently, several men who, I believe, were policemen in plain clothes, also endeavoured to lift my dress. As a consequence, three days later, I had to receive medical attention from Dr Eade, as my breasts were discoloured and very painful.

3 Later I found myself near Westminster Bridge, where Mrs Saul Solomon was valiantly struggling against the crowd, for although there were many constables near her, and an inspector, it seemed to me that instead of protecting her from the mob – a position one would have thought her age merited, if nothing else – they offered her no assistance, but rather aided the rough element in the crowd in pushing and knocking her – these men, one felt convinced, were more than merely onlookers.

Enquiry source 2B

5.5 This press photograph was taken on 18 November 1910, 'Black Friday'. The editor of the *Daily Mirror* chose the photograph for the paper's front page the following day. The Metropolitan Commissioner of Police tried to stop publication, but he failed and 750,000 copies were circulated.

Background information to Source 2B: An eyewitness reported that the police picked out a suffragette called Ada Wright. They knocked her down a couple of times and, when she came to, the bystander and another lady helped her to her feet, only to see two policemen dragging her along until she fell again. At this point a gentleman in a top hat intervened. As Ada lay on the ground with the gentleman shielding her, the press photographer Victor Console photographed her and submitted the photograph to the *Daily Mirror*.

Enquiry source 2C

The facts which gradually came to our knowledge regarding the behaviour of the police towards members of the Women's Social and Political Union on November 18, 22 and 23 [there were further demonstrations on these days] have induced us to collect the testimony of women who took part in these demonstrations, and of eye-witnesses.

The police were instructed to refrain as far as possible from making arrests. The consequence of this was that for many hours they were engaged in an incessant struggle with the police. They were flung hither and thither among moving traffic, and into the hands of a crowd permeated by plain clothes detectives, which was sometimes rough and indecent.

Continued overleaf...

Enquiry source 2C continued . . .

We cannot resist the conclusion that the police as a whole were under the impression that their duty was not merely to frustrate the attempts of the women to reach the House [of Commons] but also to terrorize them in the process. They used in numerous instances excessive violence, which was at once deliberate and aggressive, and was intended to inflict injury and pain. They frequently handled the women with gross indecency. Twenty-nine [of the 135 statements submitted to the Committee] complain of more or less aggravated acts of indecency [by the police].

We claim that the evidence here collected suffices to justify our demand for a public enquiry into the behaviour of the Metropolitan Police. The object of such an enquiry should be to ascertain, not merely whether the charges of aggressive violence, torture, and indecency here made can be substantiated, but to ascertain under what orders the police were acting.

> From a memorandum called *Treatment of the Women's Deputation by the Police* written by H.N. Brailsford about 'Black Friday' and sent to the Home Secretary, Winston Churchill, in February 1911. H.N. Brailsford was the Secretary to the Parliamentary Conciliation Committee for Woman Suffrage.

Enquiry source 2D

There may be grounds for the belief so widely held by those who took part in these demonstrations that many of their number were indecently handled but there is no foundation for the suggestion that this was done by members of the Police Force dressed in ordinary clothes and forming part of the crowd and this can be proved.

Amongst this crowd were many undesirable and reckless persons quite capable of indulging in gross conduct. The organisers are responsible for their presence as they specially invited the public by messages chalked on the footways and by leaflets to be present.

There are five allegations that constables behaved improperly. No particulars are given to enable one to identify the constables alleged to have committed these acts. I need hardly say that any such conduct on the part of a constable would be universally reprobated by the Police Service, and when the police were told on parade of this charge they were naturally very indignant.

For weeks past the official organ of the WSPU has published a notice inviting persons who could make statements as to police misconduct on 18 November and subsequent dates to place themselves in communication with Mr Brailsford and this probably accounts for the number received. There can be no doubt that these various accusations are brought forward with the object of embarrassing the authorities and of fettering police action in the future.

The police are even accused of using their heavy helmets to batter the women. I have had a helmet with all its trappings weighed and find that it is only 3.5 ounces heavier than an ordinary silk hat. What may have happened is that when a constable's helmet was knocked off by a woman he, in his convulsive effort to secure it, may have struck someone with it, but not necessarily intentionally, and certainly a helmet that weights only 11 ounces cannot be considered heavy.

Lastly I would point out that although over 200 women were brought to the Police Station and charged, there was not a single complaint made at the time of undue violence or misconduct on the part of the police, and no medical attention was needed by any of the women. It is difficult to understand why, if they had been treated as they now allege, they did not complain at the time.

> Draft memorandum written by Edward Henry, Commissioner of the Metropolitan Police, on allegations contained in Mr Brailsford's memorandum

Enquiry source 2E

No fresh instructions, verbal or written, were issued to the police on or before November 18. It was my intention from the beginning of my tenure of the Home Office, to have these women removed from the scene of disorder as soon as was lawfully possible, and then to press the prosecution only of those who had committed personal assaults on the police or other serious offences.

The directions which I gave were not fully understood or carried out on November 18. I have given explicit instructions that, in the future, with a view to avoiding disagreeable scenes, for which no one is responsible but the disorderly women themselves, police officers should be told to make arrests as soon as there is lawful occasion.

I cannot but conclude without reaffirming my conviction that the Metropolitan Police behaved on 18 November with the forbearance and humanity for which they have always been distinguished, and again repudiating the unsupported allegations which have issued from that copious fountain of mendacity, the Women's Social and Political Union.

The response of the Home Secretary, Winston Churchill, to H.N. Brailsford's Memorandum. Reported in *The Times* newspaper on 11 March 1911.

Enquiry source 2F

Historians offer different interpretations of this event. Rosen excuses police cruelty by suggesting that the force brought in for this day were too inexperienced in handling suffragette demonstrations. In the past, he argues, they had been used to policing the rough and tough working-class of the East End rather than young, genteel middle-class women, and so were at a loss as to what the correct procedure might be. In addition, women, by their very femininity, were seen to provoke police violence. 'By attempting to rush through or past police lines, these women were bringing themselves repeatedly into abrupt physical contact with the police. That the police found in youthful femininity of many of their assailants an invitation to licence, does not seem, all in all, completely surprising.'

In contrast, Susan Kingsley Kent and Martha Vicinus argue that the violence directed at the suffragettes was in fact sexual abuse. The cruelty meted out by the police is seen by such historians to be a direct result of the domestic ideology of Victorian and Edwardian Britain, whereby respectable women remained in the private sphere of home while only men and prostitutes entered the public sphere of the streets. Hence, when suffragettes demonstrated outside the male parliament, they were perceived to be no better than prostitutes. Because of this, and in order to protect their public space, men were willing to permit, even encourage, 'the violation of woman's most intimate space – her body.'

From Paula Bartley *Votes for Women 1860–1928* published in 1998

PRACTICE SOURCE EVALUATION

- Study Sources 2A and 2B. How far does the evidence of Source 2B support the sworn statements given in Source 2A?

- What inferences can be drawn from the attempt of the Metropolitan Commissioner of Police to try to stop publication of the *Daily Mirror* on 19 November 1911? Discuss this in your group.

- How far does Source 2D challenge the information given in Source 2C?

- To what extent does Source 2E support Source 2D?

- With which of the historian's views expressed in Source 2F do you agree? Why? Use this as a discussion point in your group.

SKILLS BUILDER

1 Read Sources 2A, 2C and 2D.

   How far do the views expressed in Source 2D challenge Sources 2A and 2C?

2 Read Sources 2D, 2E and 2F and use your own knowledge.

   Do you agree with the view of Susan Kingsley Kent and Martha Vicinus that the police treated the suffragettes badly because they could not believe they were respectable women?

Enquiry three: How far was the death of Emily Davison exploited by the WSPU?

On 4 June 1913, Emily Davison went to watch the Derby at Epsom racecourse. As the horses thundered towards her, she slipped under the guard rails and was trampled to death by the King's horse, Anmer. She died shortly afterwards. The WSPU gave her a magnificent funeral, claiming she had died for female suffrage and was one of their martyrs. But was her death anything more than a tragic accident? How far did the WSPU exploit her death for publicity purposes?

Enquiry source 3A

On her jacket being removed, I found two suffragette flags, 1½ yards long by ¾ yards wide, each consisting of green, white and purple stripes folded up and pinned to the back of her jacket inside.

On her person was found:

- 1 purse containing three shillings and eight pence three farthings
- 1 return half of a railway ticket from Epsom to Victoria
- 2 postal orders for 2/6 and 7/6
- 8 postage stamps
- 1 key
- 1 Helper's Pass for the Suffragette Festival, Empress Rooms, High Street, Kensington, for 4 June 1913
- 1 memo book
- 1 race card
- Some envelopes and writing paper
- 1 handkerchief

Part of the official police report on the death of Emily Wilding Davison

Enquiry source 3B

Miss Davison, who was standing a few yards from me, suddenly ducked under the railings as the horses came up. This was very near Tattenham Corner, and there was a very large crowd of people on both sides of the course.

The King's horse, Anmer, came up and Miss Davison went towards it. She put up her hand, but whether it was to catch hold of the reins or to protect herself, I do not know. It was all over in a few seconds. The horse knocked the woman over with very great force, and then stumbled and fell, pitching the jockey violently onto the ground. Both he and Miss Davison were bleeding profusely, but the crowd which swarmed about them almost immediately was too much for me to see any more.

I feel sure that Miss Davison meant to stop the horse, and that she did not go on to the course in the belief that the race was over, for, as I say, only a few of the horses had gone by when I first saw her leave the railings, and others had not passed when she was knocked down. I could not see whether any other horses touched her, for the whole thing happened so quickly, and I was so horrified at seeing her pitched violently down by the horse that I did not think of anything. The affair distressed the crowd very much.

From an eyewitness, John Ervine

Enquiry source 3C

Emily Davison and a fellow-militant in whose flat she lived, had planned a Derby protest without tragedy – a mere waving of the purple-white-and-green at Tattenham Corner, which, by its suddenness, it was hoped would stop the race. Whether from the first her purpose was more serious, or whether a final impulse altered her resolve, I know not. Her friend declares that she would not thus have deliberately died without writing a farewell message to her mother. Yet, she sewed the WSPU colours inside her coat as though to ensure that no mistake could be made as to her motive when her body should be examined.

From Sylvia Pankhurst *The Suffrage Movement: An Intimate Account of Persons and Ideals* published in 1931

Enquiry source 3D

5.6 A photograph of Emily Davison's funeral procession in London on 14 June 1913. Suffragettes, dressed in white, carrying wreaths and a purple silk banner, accompanied the hearse.

Enquiry source 3E

She was the first to talk about dying for the cause. Her suicide was a brave act, but foolish and unnecessary; it had little effect on the 'Votes for Women' movement, except to confirm for many that a sensible idea had become exaggerated out of all proportion.

From D.C. Brooks *The Emancipation of Women* published in 1970

SKILLS BUILDER

1 Study Sources 3A, 3B and 3C.

   To what extent do these sources support the view that Emily Davison deliberately made herself a martyr for the suffragette cause?

2 Study Sources 3C, 3D and 3E and use your own knowledge.

   How far do you agree with the view that Emily Davison's act was 'foolish and unnecessary'?

Unit summary

What have you learned in this unit?

Militancy gradually increased in intensity and type throughout the period 1903–14. The strategies and tactics developed by the suffragettes gained the oxygen of publicity for the cause, gaining support from some as well as alienating others. The WSPU itself was organised on an hierarchical basis, with the Pankhursts at the apex of the triangle. This undemocratic structure was criticised by some, but others remained convinced that it was the only way to deliver a swift and rapid response to government actions. Although the militant suffragettes tended to gain most of the publicity after about 1903–4, the constitutional suffragists continued their work of persuasion and argument.

What skills have you used in this unit?

Your evaluation of the source material will have helped develop your understanding of the changing nature of the militant campaign and you will have assessed the importance of specific individuals to the changing nature of that campaign.

Biography

Emmeline Pankhurst (1857–1928)

Born in Manchester in 1858, Emmeline's parents (Robert Goulden and Sophia Crane) held radical political beliefs and Emmeline was taken to women's suffrage meetings in the 1870s. In 1879 she married Richard Pankhurst. A committed socialist and an advocate of women's suffrage, he had been responsible for the drafting of the Married Women's Property Acts of 1870 and 1882. He died in 1898. They had four children: Christabel (1880); Sylvia (1882); Frank (1884); and Adela (1885). Emmeline:

- 1889 helped form the pressure group the Women's Franchise League;
- 1895 became a Poor Law guardian;
- 1903 founded the Women's Social and Political Union;
- 1905 encouraged the WSPU to embark on alternative methods to obtain the vote;
- 1907 moved to London and joined her two daughters in the struggle for female enfranchisement and used escalating militancy to obtain this end;
- was arrested, imprisoned and force-fed many times;
- 1914 stopped all activities to achieve female enfranchisement and focused on the war effort;
- wrote her autobiography *My Story* in 1914;
- claimed responsibility for the 1918 and 1928 Acts that enfranchised women.

Biography

Christabel Pankhurst (1880–1958)

- first child and eldest daughter of Richard and Emmeline Pankhurst, attended Manchester High School;
- 1901 met Eva Gore-Booth who was trying to persuade working-class women in Manchester to join the NUWSS;
- 1903 with her mother, Emmeline, formed the WSPU;
- 1905 arrested and imprisoned, with Annie Kenny, for disrupting a Liberal Party meeting;
- 1907 obtained a law degree from Manchester University but couldn't take it because she was a woman;
- advocated a campaign that moved away from working-class women and focused on the middle-class and the wealthy;
- favoured a limited suffrage that would give the vote only to women with money and property;
- gained control of the WSPU in London;
- 1912 fled to France when police clamped down on individual members of the WSPU;
- 1912–14 edited *The Suffragette*;
- 1914 all suffragettes released from prison and WSPU ended militant activities.

Biography

Annie Kenney (1879–1953)

Born in Springhead, near Oldham, one of eleven children. Her parents worked in the Oldham textile industry. Aged 10, she worked part-time in the Woodend Mill and full-time from the age of 13. Joined the local branch of the ILP, where she heard Christabel Pankhurst speak on women's rights and the two women became close friends.

Joined WSPU:

1905	arrested with Christabel, and imprisoned, for interrupting a Liberal Party meeting;
1905–14	imprisoned several times for illegal activities trying to get votes for women;
1912	took over leadership of WSPU;
1914	ended militant activities; campaigned for women to be allowed to work in munitions factories;
1924	published autobiography *Memories of a Millhand*;
1926	married James Taylor and withdrew from public life.

RESEARCH TASK

Sylvia Pankhurst

In Trafalgar Square, London, there are four huge granite plinths. One is empty: it has no statue on it. Many people have suggested that a statue of Sylvia Pankhurst should be erected on this empty plinth. Research her life and contribution to society, and make an argued case either in favour or against this suggestion.

6 The women's suffrage question: action and reaction

What is this unit about?

This unit focuses on the reaction of various elements in society to the suffrage campaigns in the years between 1906, when the Liberal Party won a landslide victory, to the outbreak of war in 1914. The most important element, of course, was the Liberal government that was in power throughout these years. But other elements were influential, too, in changing attitudes and in their support for, or opposition to, those seeking votes for women. In this unit you will find out about:

- the reaction of the Liberal government;
- the attitudes of the Conservative and Labour parties;
- the response of the churches, the media and the trade unions;

to the suffrage campaigns.

Key questions

- How far did the attitudes of those in positions of influence towards the suffrage campaigns change in the years 1906–14?
- What impact did the militant campaigns have on changing people's attitudes towards the enfranchisement of women?

Timeline

1906	Liberal Party won landslide election victory
1908	Women's Suffrage Bill carried by 179 votes
1909	second reading of Electoral Reform Bill, which included votes for women
	suffragettes banned from Liberal meetings
	government ordered the forcible feeding of hunger striking suffragettes
1910	Conciliation Bill carried by 139 votes
1911	May: second Conciliation Bill debated
	November: failure of second Conciliation Bill
1912	third Conciliation Bill failed at second reading
1913	amendment to Franchise Bill ruled out of order by Speaker
	The Prisoners' Temporary Discharge for Ill-Health Act (Cat and Mouse Act) passed
1914	March: government closes galleries because the Rokeby Venus slashed by a suffragette
	August: Britain declares war on Germany
	WSPU suspended militancy

Source A

THE DIGNITY OF THE FRANCHISE.

QUALIFIED VOTER. "AH, YOU MAY PAY RATES AN' TAXES, AN' YOU MAY 'AVE RESPONSERBILITIES AN' ALL.; BUT WHEN IT COMES TO *VOTIN'*, YOU MUST LEAVE IT TO *US MEN!*"

6.1 A cartoon published in the magazine *Punch* in May 1905

Question

What do you think is the cartoonist's attitude to women's suffrage? Discuss this in your group.

Definition

Universal manhood suffrage

Giving the vote to all adult men.

The cartoonist is pointing out very sharply the situation that existed at the beginning of the twentieth century. The 1884 Reform Act added an extra 2.5 million voters to the electorate, most of whom were farm workers and rural craftsmen. Educated middle-class women were put in the position of seeing loutish workmen, like the one portrayed in this cartoon, being able to vote while they themselves could not. However, the qualifications necessary to vote still excluded many adult males and these, together with the level of literacy needed to register as a voter, meant that in effect around one third of all adult males were still disenfranchised. The vast majority of these were unskilled and casual workers. Thus any discussion concerning the enfranchisement of women was, in male eyes at least, bound up with **universal manhood suffrage**.

Why was it so difficult to gain the approval of parliamentary parties for women's suffrage?

As well as being tied up with attitudes towards universal manhood suffrage, female suffrage was viewed with apprehension by the main political parties. This was because no one knew – though they could guess – how large numbers of enfranchised women would vote. No party would want to increase the electorate in this way if it meant reducing their chances of winning a general election.

The traditional view has been that the Conservative Party disliked any extension of democracy; the Liberals were apprehensive at the prospect of extending the property-based qualification because they were convinced that property-owning women would vote Conservative; and the Labour Party generally favoured universal suffrage and were reluctant to extend the franchise only as far as to include property-owning middle-class women. However, these are broad stereotypes. As you will see, a variety of opinions and attitudes existed within all the political parties.

Why was the Liberal government reluctant to give women the vote?

The general election of 1906 resulted in a Liberal landslide. With this landslide victory, the hopes of all radical reforming groups, including those pressing for the enfranchisement of women, were raised high. A considerable number of Liberal MPs were known to be sympathetic to the women's cause, including the influential David Lloyd George. The Liberal party's initial huge majority gave the government the power to deliver votes for women. All previous bills for one form or another of female enfranchisement had been **Private Members' Bills** and they failed because of lack of government support. Would the government now find parliamentary time to support a women's suffrage bill? The short answer is 'No'. Neither suffragists nor suffragettes managed to persuade the Liberal government to support votes for women.

> **Definition**
>
> **Private Members' Bills**
>
> A bill drawn up and proposed by an individual member of parliament without any government involvement.

There would seem to be three main reasons why the Liberal government was reluctant to give women the vote:

- Herbert Asquith, who became Prime Minister in 1908, was not in favour of giving women the vote and so was not inclined to find parliamentary time in his busy reformist programme for women's suffrage.
- The Liberal government's majority was steadily reduced by a number of by-elections and, after 1910, was forced to rely on the support of Irish Nationalists and the Labour Party to remain in power. It was not, therefore, likely to be willing to introduce an issue that was so controversial that its majority could be wiped out.

- The Liberals had other, far more important problems with which to grapple: insurrection in Ireland; industrial unrest and a rebellious House of Lords.

But these could be seen as excuses. The Liberals, as a parliamentary party, were ambiguous about women's suffrage and refused, as a party, to endorse it. Each time the issue was raised, the government skilfully cut the ground from beneath the feet of women's suffrage supporters. The source by Paula Bartley provides a catalogue of failed attempts and the reasons for their failure.

Source B

The Liberal Government and Votes for Women

1906	Government refused to support an amendment to a Plural Voting bill, which would have enfranchised a number of propertied women
1907	Women's Suffrage Bill rejected
1908	Women's Suffrage Bill carried
1909	Second reading of Women's Suffrage Bill carried, but Asquith refused to support it and so the bill failed
1910	First Conciliation Bill carried but ultimately fell because the government failed to give it parliamentary time
1911	Second Conciliation Bill carried but Asquith announced that he preferred to support manhood suffrage but which could include an amendment for the enfranchisement of women
1913	Government Franchise Bill introduced universal male suffrage but an amendment to include women was declared unconstitutional.

From Paula Bartley *Votes for Women 1860–1928* in published in 1998

Question

Why was Asquith so opposed to giving women the vote?

Time and time again, it seemed, women were being led to believe that female enfranchisement was within their grasp, only to have it snatched away by a two-faced government.

The Liberal leader, Henry Campbell-Bannerman, was a man who had privately always been sympathetic to female suffrage although he opposed it publicly. He might, therefore, have been won round were it not for ill-health that forced his resignation. He was succeeded in 1908 as party leader and Prime Minister by Herbert Asquith. Asquith had set his face against female suffrage since the 1880s and the campaign for votes for women faced a difficult time.

Source C

6.2 A photograph of a rally 'Votes for Women' organised by the WSPU in 1908. From the start, they realised that Asquith was going to be the main obstacle to women's suffrage.

Source D

Asquith's stubbornness requires some explanation since he persisted to the point where his opposition had begun to damage both the party's interests and his own standing as Leader. Though sometimes portrayed as aloof from party politics, Asquith was in reality a narrowly partisan figure, ever fearful of conceding an advantage to his opponents. Moreover, despite his relatively humble origins, he had acquired an elitist outlook, lacked sympathy with those he regarded as mediocre or ill-educated, and lost touch with his provincial origins in his enjoyment of Balliol College [Oxford University], the law and London society. He therefore found it difficult to understand why ordinary women wanted the vote so badly. This bias was reinforced by Asquith's own experience which led him to treat women essentially as amiable companions and uncritical supporters. His two wives*, in their different ways, confirmed this. Helen had no interest in politics, while Margot showed far too much! Asquith so feared Margot's interference and wild indiscretions that he tried to keep her in ignorance of higher politics altogether.

From Martin Pugh *The March of the Women* published in 2000

* Asquith's first wife was Helen Melland. She died of typhoid fever in 1891 while on holiday in Scotland. Asquith's second wife was Emma Tennant (Margot) whom he married in 1894. Asquith had seven children: five from his first marriage and two from his second.

Question

How believable do you find Martin Pugh's explanation as to why Asquith was so opposed to giving women the vote? How would an historian set about uncovering a politician's motive for doing something?

Definitions

People's Budget

A budget introduced in 1909 by the Chancellor of the Exchequer, David Lloyd George. In it he funded both old age pensions (an entirely new idea) and a Dreadnought battleship building programme by imposing new taxes on the rich. This enraged the Conservative Party (who had a majority in the House of Lords) and precipitated a constitutional crisis when the Lords rejected the budget.

The Irish Question

In the nineteenth and twentieth centuries, the 'Irish Question' focused on whether to give Home Rule to the whole island of Ireland, or to divide the island into Ulster and Eire or to continue to rule the whole island from Westminster.

How significant were the Conciliation Bills?

1910 was a tricky year for the government. Desperate to force his **People's Budget** through parliament, Chancellor David Lloyd George put the government on a collision course with the House of Lords. The government won, in the sense that the power of the Lords was curbed, but there was a price to pay. Two general elections in one year (January and December) resulted in the loss, to the Liberal government, of its overall majority. Indeed, they were kept in power by the combined votes of the Irish Nationalists and the Labour Party. The Irish Nationalists, looking for a settlement of **The Irish Question**, were not minded to support parliamentary time being given to women's suffrage. The Labour Party, as we have seen, were more in favour of universal suffrage than debating whether or not to give the vote to women of property, and at this point in time they were preoccupied with a series of industrial disputes.

Then pressure from supporters of votes for women took a different turn.

Source E

I have some thought of attempting to found a Conciliation Committee for Women's Suffrage. My idea is that it should undertake the necessary diplomatic work of promoting an early settlement. It should not be large, and should consist of both men and women – the women in touch with the existing societies but not their more prominent leaders, the men also as far as possible not identified officially with either party.

Part of a letter from the journalist and suffragist, Henry Brailsford, to Millicent Fawcett, written on 18 January 1910

By the spring of 1910 a Conciliation Committee, consisting of fifty-four suffragist MPs from all parties had come into being. The Chairman was the Earl of Lytton, and the Honorary Secretary, Henry Brailsford. The WSPU suspended militant activities and all women's suffrage groups set aside their differences and supported the Conciliation Bills.

Source F

1 Every woman possessed of a household qualification within the meaning of the Representation of the People Act (1884), shall be entitled to be registered as a voter, and when registered to vote in the county or borough in which the qualifying premises are situate.
2 For the purposes of this Act, a woman shall not be disqualified by marriage, for being registered as a vote, provided that a husband and wife shall not both be registered as voters in the same parliamentary borough or county division.
3 This Act may be cited as the Representation of the People Act, 1911.

Part of the draft Conciliation Bill introduced in the summer of 1910 and again in May 1911

Source G

> **YOU want**
> VOTES FOR WOMEN HOUSEHOLDERS?
>
> # FOLLOW THE CROWD
> TO ALEXANDRA PARK, SATURDAY OCT. 8
>
> ## Gigantic Joint Demonstration
>
> **Six Platforms**
> Women's Freedom League, Women's Social & Political Union, Women Workers, Men's Political Union for Women's Enfranchisement, Men's League for Women's Suffrage Education, National Association of Midwives, Upholsterers' Union, Leather Workers' Union, Cigarette Makers' Union, Fawcett Debating Society
>
> **TWENTY SPEAKERS**
>
> **ALL PARTIES SUPPORT THE CONCILIATION BILL**

6.3 Words from a suffrage flier, distributed in Manchester in 1910

Source H

6.4 A photograph of a WSPU rally in support of the Conciliation Bill

Question

Does anything about this photograph surprise you? Discuss this in your group.

The Conciliation Bill received a parliamentary majority of 109 in July 1910. Under pressure from his cabinet colleagues, the most of whom were in favour of female enfranchisement, Asquith agreed to give the bill parliamentary time. A second general election intervened and the bill was reintroduced in May 1911, when it passed with a resounding majority of 255 to 88. After a heated discussion, the Cabinet agreed to give the Conciliation bill one week of government time. Yet women did not get the vote in 1911. So what went wrong?

Source I

Prominent Liberals condemned the bill as fundamentally detrimental to the party's interests. Churchill complained that it gave 'an entirely unfair representation to property as against persons'; Lloyd George complained that it 'would, on balance, add hundreds of thousands of votes to the strength of the Conservative party'; and when ministers asked the Chief Whip to consult the various regional Liberal federations they largely backed up this diagnosis with dire warnings: 'suicidal to pass the bill . . . would wipe out Liberal representation . . . nobody wants it and everybody dreads its advent.' None of this excitable comment should be taken as proof of the impact of the bill, but nor can it be ignored as a partial explanation for what subsequently happened.

From Martin Pugh *The March of Women* published in 2000

Source J

The Liberal party ought to make up its mind whether it will either have an extended franchise which would put the working men's wives on to the register as well as spinsters and widows, or that it will have no female franchise at all.

Part of a letter from David Lloyd George to the Scottish Master of Elibank, written on 5 September 1911

Prime Minister Asquith, heartened by these divisions, for once took the initiative. He announced that he was in favour of a manhood suffrage bill that although would not specifically include female enfranchisement, would not exclude it either. Suffragists would be able to propose an amendment that would enable women, or some women, to vote. To many Liberals this seemed the ideal way forward. The second Conciliation Bill was finally defeated and all efforts were concentrated on devising an acceptable amendment to the proposed government sponsored reform bill. Millicent Fawcett, the leader of the NUWSS, held confidential talks with Sir Edward Grey, the foreign secretary who was a leading Liberal suffragist, the Women's Liberal Federation held a major rally and Lloyd George was enthusiastic 'Our success next year, I think, is assured. I do not see what there is to prevent it.' He had counted without the Speaker of the House of Commons. In a totally unprecedented move, Speaker James Lowther refused to accept an amendment concerning women's suffrage. The government promptly abandoned its own bill.

Disillusioned by what they saw as deception and duplicity on the part of the government in general and Asquith in particular, members of the NUWSS left the Women's Liberal Federation in droves and many began to focus their support on the Labour Party. The WSPU returned to violence. Their truce was over.

Source K

"SERMONS IN STONES."

John Bull (to *Non-militant Suffragist*). "I COULD LISTEN MORE ATTENTIVELY, MADAM, TO YOUR PLEAS, WERE IT NOT FOR THESE CONCRETE ARGUMENTS WHICH I FIND RATHER DISTRACTING."

6.5 A cartoon published in the magazine *Punch* in November 1911

SKILLS BUILDER

How valid is the attitude to militancy shown in this cartoon?

How successfully did the Liberal government deal with suffragette militancy?

The Liberal government (see pages 60–3), had at first responded to violence by arresting the suffragettes causing the disturbances. Originally their offences were relatively mild, but the suffragettes refused to pay the fines meted out by magistrates and there was no option but to imprison them. The spectacle of respectable middle-class women entering prison was not one the government welcomed. But this was one the suffragettes wanted.

Source L

6.6 A photograph of Mary Leigh (left) and Edith New (right) on their release from Holloway prison on 22 August 1908. The two women, who had given up their teaching careers to work with the WSPU, had broken windows in Downing Street on 30 June 1908. They were sentenced to two months in prison.

Question

Why might the Liberal government not have been too happy with this reaction to their punishment of suffragettes? Discuss this in your group.

At first, women prisoners were given 'First Division' treatment, which meant that they had the status of political prisoners, were allowed to wear their own clothes and receive food parcels. After 1908, however, suffragettes were placed in the 'Second Division' and were treated as ordinary criminals. The following year, suffragette Marion Wallace Dunlop decided to take a different approach. She refused all food. Hunger striking then became the weapon of choice for imprisoned suffragettes.

At first, hunger strikers were released from prison. Then the government, terrified of having a suffragette die in prison and anxious not to create martyrs, introduced forcible feeding for hunger-striking suffragettes. Over a thousand women were forcibly fed through their nostrils, mouths and even through the rectum and the vagina. Nevertheless, the government chose its victims carefully. Lady Constance Lytton, a vigorous suffragette, had always been medically examined when arrested, declared to be too ill to undergo forced feeding, and released. Disguised as a working-class woman, Joan Wharton, she was offered no such release but was force-fed seven times. This enabled the WSPU to draw attention to class divisions in prison and society at large that would, they claimed, be ended when women got the vote.

The suffragettes submitted willingly to this treatment. Disgusting and humiliating though it was, it made great publicity for the cause. The Liberal government found that its actions were turned into publicity stunts and used against it in electioneering.

Source M

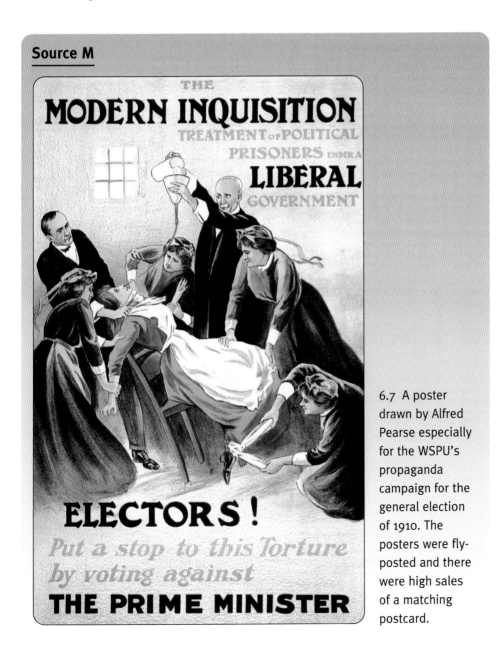

6.7 A poster drawn by Alfred Pearse especially for the WSPU's propaganda campaign for the general election of 1910. The posters were fly-posted and there were high sales of a matching postcard.

Source N

Prisoners were held down by force, flung on the floor, tied to chairs and iron bedsteads while the tube was forced up the nostrils. After each feeding the pain gets worse. The wardress endeavoured to make the prisoner open her mouth by sawing the edge of the cup along her gums. The broken edge caused laceration and severe pain. Food into the lung of one unresisting prisoner immediately produced severe choking, vomiting and persistent coughing. She was hurriedly released next day suffering from pneumonia and pleurisy. We cannot believe that any of our colleagues will agree that this form of prison treatment is justly described in Mr McKenna's [Home Secretary] word as necessary medical treatment.

From the medical journal *The Lancet* published in August 1912

Adverse publicity about forced feeding, such as that shown in Source N, caused the government to think again. In 1913, parliament passed the Prisoners' Temporary Discharge for Ill-Health Act. This permitted prison authorities to release hunger strikers when they became weak and ill so as to give them time to recover, at which point they would be promptly re-arrested. Unsurprisingly, the WSPU dubbed this the 'Cat and Mouse' Act and launched a scathing publicity campaign. It failed to move the Home Secretary, Reginald McKenna.

Source O

I have had unlimited correspondence from every section of the public who have been good enough to advise me as to what I ought to do, and among them all I have not been able to discover more than four alternative methods. The first is to let them die. That is, I should say, at the present moment, the most popular judging by the number of letters I have received. The second is to deport them. The third is to treat them as lunatic, and the fourth is to give them the franchise. I think we should not adopt any of them.

Said by Home Secretary Reginald McKenna in debate in the House of Commons on 11 June 1914. Here he is reflecting on suffragette hunger strikers.

So, overall, was the government hostile to female enfranchisement? On the surface, it would seem so. Historian Paula Bartley digs deeper.

Source P

The response of the government to women who broke the law certainly suggests it was hostile to votes for women. There was a decided contrast between the treatment of law-breaking Ulster Unionists (who made inflammatory speeches and smuggled in guns) and law-breaking suffragettes. A blind eye was turned to the gun smuggling. Ulster rebels were not arrested. Instead, they were consulted by the government. The suffragettes, on the other hand, were first ignored, then harassed, arrested, imprisoned and force-fed. When the WSPU began its illegal activities, the government reacted by denying them democratic forms of protest. Women were forbidden to attend Liberal meetings unless they had a signed ticket. The government refused to meet delegations or accept petitions. It banned public meetings and censored the Press in an attempt to silence the WSPU. The Commissioner of Police (directed by the Home Office) refused to allow suffragettes to meet in parks in London. Eventually, the management agreed not to hire out the Albert Hall to suffragettes. When the WSPU found another venue, the government threatened to remove the owner's licence. The government also prosecuted the Suffragette's printer and raided the offices and homes of WSPU members.

From Paula Bartley *Votes for Women 1860–1928* published in 1998

Question

Why do you think the government acted in such an oppressive way to suffragettes and not to other law-breakers?

To what extent did the Conservative Party support votes for women?

What was the attitude of the parliamentary Conservative Party?

The Conservative Party was as divided over women's suffrage as the Liberal Party, and even individuals seemed to say and think different things at different times:

- In 1866, Disraeli said 'I do not see on what reasons she has not a right to vote.' But when John Stuart Mill proposed an amendment to the 1867 Reform Bill that would have enfranchised women, Disraeli gave him no support at all.

- In 1881, Lord Salisbury maintained 'The day is not far distant when women will also bear their share in voting for members of parliament and in determining the policy of the country.' But he voted against a second reading of a women's suffrage bill in 1891.

- Conservatives in the House of Lords were generally opposed to giving women the vote. However, Lord Lytton (Constance Lytton's brother, see page 91) was president of the Men's League for Women's Suffrage and consistently supported female enfranchisement in the House of Lords. On the other hand, Lords Cromer and Curzon were presidents of the Anti-Suffrage League.

- In 1892, Arthur Balfour pointed out the implicit contradiction in 'giving a vote to a man who contributes nothing to taxation but what he pays on his beer, while you refuse enfranchisement to a woman whatever her contribution to the state may be.' But as leader of the Conservative Party and Prime Minister, he did nothing to encourage female suffrage.

- Some Conservative MPs worked on the Conciliation Committee (see page 87).
- In 1913, Bonar Law, following Balfour as leader of the Conservative Party, refused to support an amendment to a franchise reform bill that would have enfranchised women.

The Conservative Party was generally opposed, after Disraeli's **'leap in the dark'** in 1867, to any extension of the franchise, and it does seem that any opposition to votes for women was because of this, not because they were particularly opposed to women voters. Indeed, at their annual conferences, the National Union of Conservative Associations voted seven times in the years 1887 and 1910, for female enfranchisement.

What was the attitude of Conservative women in the country at large?

The work of the Primrose League (see page 38) does seem to have supported the cause of female suffrage.

Source Q

In the long run, the Primrose League surely assisted rather than retarded the cause of women's enfranchisement in spite of not being a suffragist organisation, indeed perhaps because of it; for the League steadily undermined assumptions about political inertia and ignorance of women without driving men as a whole into opposition. An apprenticeship in organisations like the League was for many British women a pre-condition for their subsequent suffragism.

From Martin Pugh *The Tories and the People 1880–1935* published 1985

How far did the Labour Party support women's suffrage?

The Labour Party emerged as a major force in British politics in the years 1903–14. It might at first seem natural that a party of the left would automatically embrace the cause of women's suffrage. However, although a solid core of Labour MPs voted consistently for female enfranchisement, this was not generally the case. The problem for the Labour Party, with its socialist principles, was that it favoured universal suffrage. Faced with pressure from middle-class women wanting the vote on equal terms with men (remember that roughly 60 per cent of working-class men were excluded from the franchise) many Labour MPs simply thought that they would be perpetuating the class system they had vowed to destroy. So it was quite common to find women's suffrage being dismissed as a middle-class concern, but as something that would automatically happen once universal suffrage was achieved.

What was the attitude of the parliamentary Labour Party?

Source R

I have no objection to revolution, if it is necessary, but I have the very strongest objection to childishness masquerading as revolution, and all I can say of these window-breaking expeditions is that they are simply silly and provocative. I wish the working women of the country, who really care for the vote, would come to London and tell these pettifogging middle-class damsels who are going out with little hammers in their muffs that if they do not go home they will get their heads broken.

Ramsay MacDonald, a future leader of the Labour Party and Prime Minister, was sympathetic to the cause of women's suffrage, but critical of the suffragettes

On the other hand, Keir Hardie, the first leader of the Labour Party in the Commons, was close to the Pankhursts and supported the militant campaign, collecting funds, writing leaflets and teaching them about parliamentary techniques. The Labour MP George Lansbury was a strong supporter of the WSPU. In 1912 he proposed that Labour MPs vote against the government on all bills until women had the vote. He resigned his seat, hoping to be re-elected on his pro-women's suffrage stance. Despite being supported in his election campaign by both the WSPU and the NUWSS, he lost.

What was the attitude of the Labour Party in the country at large?

The WSPU received the active support of many Labour Party branches. The Woolwich branch, for example, consistently supported the aims and methods of the WSPU. Members appreciated that even a limited franchise would give the vote to a number of working-class widows and spinsters who happened to be householders.

1912 – a significant turning point?

In 1912, two events occurred that seemed to indicate that the Labour Party as a whole was moving towards wholehearted support of women's suffrage.

1 At the Labour Party's annual January conference, Arthur Henderson proposed that the party should only support an adult suffrage bill if it enfranchised women as well. This proposal was accepted by the delegates.

2 The NUWSS dropped its opposition to allying with a political party and formed an election pact with the Labour Party. This meant that they raised a special fund and designated election organisers not only to help Labour MPs retain their seats, but to assist Labour candidates in seats where the sitting Liberal MP was anti-female suffrage.

Question

Why do you think the NUWSS would have entered into this pact with the Labour Party?

How far did religious institutions, the media and trade unions support women's suffrage?

The three main political parties were, as you have seen, very mixed in their support of and opposition to, women's suffrage. It was the same with the other three bastions of male supremacy: the trade unions, the churches and the media.

The trade unions

The trade union movement, as a whole, was generally hostile to women's suffrage. The 1901 Trades Union Congress showed themselves to be antagonistic to votes for women and in 1912 the National Union of Mineworkers, with their large block vote, successfully opposed a motion calling for votes for women.

However:

- there were some women's trade unions (see page 162)
- several weavers' unions in Lancashire encouraged their MPs to support women's suffrage and petitioned parliament in support
- in the east end of London, Sylvia Pankhurst drew massive support from large numbers of unionised working-class men
- Glasgow dockers supported the WSPU.

Indeed, in 1913, the TUC followed the Labour Party in agreeing that support for suffrage reform should only be given if that reform included enfranchising women.

Religious institutions

Religious institutions tended to be, as with other male-dominated institutions, very mixed in their reactions to the women's suffrage question. It is known that the Chief Rabbi was pro-female enfranchisement, as, generally, were non-conformists and Quakers. Labour churches were founded in Manchester and invited leading suffragists to speak to their congregations; Quaker men and women enjoyed equality, with both sexes having equal rights to speak at meetings. The established Church of England, however, managed to maintain something of a silence on the subject and for this they were castigated by the WSPU.

Source S

We indict the Church with having aided and abetted the State in robbing women of the vote. The Church is thus held guilty of the subjection of women and all the vice, suffering and social degradation that result from that subjection. Whereas it is the duty of the Church to insist upon the political enfranchisement of women – not only as a political reform, but as a moral and even a religious reform – the Church has actually boycotted this great question and has condoned the torture of the women who are fighting for their liberty.

From the WSPU's *Annual Report* published in 1914

On the other hand, a number of churchmen did not deserve such criticism.

Source T

The extension of the suffrage to women seems to me a logical sequence of Christian principle. In the Christian society there is no superior sex, the equality of each member is recognised, the individuality of each person is sacred. St Paul asserted this when he wrote 'in baptism there is neither male nor female.' The rights of each are equal, therefore women are entitled to express their convictions and assert their individuality by voting if they choose to do so.

From *Opinions of Leaders of Religious Thought* published by the Central Society for Women's Suffrage in 1905. Here the Rector of Whitburn expresses his opinion.

The media

Newspapers report the news, but then as now they have to please their proprietors and keep an eye on circulation figures. Nevertheless, as a general rule, national newspapers were hostile to women's suffrage. Indeed, they did not begin to get seriously interested until the campaign became militant and therefore newsworthy.

- *The Times* was steadfastly hostile to women's suffrage and published letters that agreed with the newspaper's general attitude.

- The *London Standard* followed a similar line, condemning suffragettes as 'deranged lunatics'.

- The *Daily Mirror* published the photographs of Black Friday, as did the *Illustrated London News*. But did this indicate support for the WSPU or a desire to increase circulation by printing titillating photographs? The *Daily Mirror*, however, had been founded by Lord Northcliffe specifically to appeal to women.

- *The Workman's Times* supported votes for women and some men produced their own papers in support of women's suffrage. In 1905 J. Francis, for example, started a weekly *Women's Franchise.*

- Some local papers, closer to individuals living and working in their localities and with a better understanding of local dynamics, tended to be more sympathetic to the suffrage cause. The *Lewisham Borough News,* for example, was sympathetic to the suffragists but not the suffragettes.

- The magazine *Punch* displayed considerable exasperation with the tactics of the Asquith government and the vast majority of the cartoons it published on the subject of women's suffrage were supportive of the cause.

It must be remembered that, for both suffragists and suffragettes, almost any publicity was good publicity, bringing 'the cause' to the public's attention on a regular basis.

Both suffragists and suffragettes published their own newspapers and journals in an attempt to get their message across to supporters and doubters alike, for example:

- the NUWSS published *Common Cause*;
- the Women's Franchise League published *Vote*;
- the WSPU published *Votes for Women* and *The Suffragette*;
- Sylvia Pankhurst published the *Dreadnought*.

Positives in the negative?

This unit's main focus has been on the actions and reactions of the Liberal government. This is because, ultimately, any decision to enfranchise women had to have the support of whichever political party was in power. Historian Martin Pugh finds some merit in the Asquith government's approach.

Definition

Veto powers of the House of Lords

One outcome of the constitutional crisis precipitated by the House of Lords' rejection of the People's Budget (see page 86) was the Parliament Act of 1911. By this Act the House of Lords could no longer veto bills: it could only delay them.

Source U

The prolonged confrontation between Asquith's government and the suffragists had not been wholly barren of results. It had established what ought to have been accepted earlier, that votes for women could not be treated simply as a question of principle but had to be translated into a form acceptable to the governing party. The vital achievement of Asquith's administration lay in the removal of the ultimate obstacle to the women's vote – the **veto powers of the House of Lords**.

From Martin Pugh *The March of the Women* published in 2000

Enquiry four: What was the nature and impact of the anti-suffragist campaign?

There were many private and public expressions of hostility towards giving the vote to women. However, it was not until the beginning of the twentieth century that opponents of women's suffrage began to organise. Anti-suffrage groups were formed up and down the country, some with a local focus and some aiming for national impact. For example, in July 1908 the Women's National Anti-Suffrage League was formed, with Lady Jersey as the chair of the executive committee and Mrs Humphrey Ward as the driving force behind the campaigning. Five month's later the national Men's Committee for Opposing Female Suffrage was launched. In 1910 the two groups amalgamated into the National League for Opposing Women's Suffrage.

Enquiry source 4A

As might be expected, the Anti-Suffrage League adopted a non-party stance and constitutional tactics. It worked behind the scenes, lobbying waverers in the Commons and maintaining pressure on known Antis in all parties. More publicly it produced anti-suffrage propaganda and held meetings to publicise its point of view. The style was very different from that of the suffragists. The Anti-Suffrage League could offer none of Mrs Pankhurst's drama and flamboyance, none of Mrs Fawcett's intelligent perception of women's problems, none of the imaginativeness and inventiveness in campaigning methods which lent such panache to Edwardian suffragism. On the other hand, Antis did not want these things. They wanted a well organised, discreet and politically informed leadership which could work successfully within the political elite and mobilise already existing anti-suffrage sentiment in the country at large.

From B. Harrison *Separate Spheres: The Opposition to Women's Suffrage in Britain* published in 1978

Enquiry source 4B

He had always contended that if we opened the door and enfranchised ever so small a number of females, they could not possibly close it, and that it ultimately meant adult suffrage. The government of the country would therefore be handed over to a majority who would not be men, but women. Women are creatures of impulse and emotion and did not decide questions on the grounds of reason, as men did.

He was sometimes described as a woman-hater, but he had had two wives, and he thought that was the best answer he could give to those who called him a woman-hater. He was too fond of them to drag them into the political arena and to ask them to undertake responsibilities, duties and obligations which they did not understand and did not care for.

What did one find when one got into the company of women and talked politics? They were soon asked to stop talking silly politics, and yet that was the type of people to whom we are invited to hand over the destinies of the country.

It was not only because he thought that women were unfitted by their physical nature to exercise political power, but because he believed that the majority of them did not want it and would vote against it, that he asked the House to pause before they took the step suggested by the honourable member for Merthyr Tydfil (Keir Hardie). He believed that if women were enfranchised the end would be disastrous to all political parties. He therefore asked the House to pause before it took a step from which it could never retreat.

Part of a report in *Hansard* on the speech made by William Cremer in the House of Commons on 25 April 1906. William Cremer later became one of the presidents of the Men's Committee for Opposing Female Suffrage.

Enquiry source 4C

Votes for Women

While in the act of voting, M.rs Jones remembers that she has left a cake in the oven!

6.8 An anti-suffrage postcard produced in 1908

Enquiry source 4D

Women's suffrage is a more dangerous leap in the dark than it was in the 1860s because of the vast growth of the Empire, the immense increase of England's imperial responsibilities and therewith the increased complexity and risk of the problems which lie before our statesmen – constitutional, legal, financial, military, international problems – problems of men, only to be solved by the labour and special knowledge of men, and where the men who bear the burden ought to be left unhampered by the political inexperience of women.

Part of a letter written by Mrs Humphrey Ward and published in *The Times* on 27 February 1909

Enquiry source 4E

There was a large attendance at an 'At Home' held at Hurst-on-Clays, East Grinstead, by kind permission of Lady Jeannie Lucinda Musgrave on Tuesday afternoon. Mrs Archibald Colquhoun of the Women's National Anti-Suffrage League said that women had never possessed the right to vote for members of parliament in this country, nor in any great country, and although the right to vote had been granted in one or two smaller countries, such as Australia and New Zealand, no great empire had given women a voice in running the country. Women have not had the political experience that men have and, on the whole, did not want the vote, and had little knowledge of, or interest in, politics. Politics would go on without the help of women, but the home wouldn't.

The speaker also stated that in a recent canvas by postcard, of the 200-odd women in East Grinstead, they found that 80 did not want the vote, 40 did want the vote and the remainder were not sufficiently interested to reply. Lady Musgrave, President of the East Grinstead branch of the Anti-Suffragette League said she was strongly against the franchise being extended to women, for she did not think it would do any good whatsoever, and in sex interests, would do a lot of harm. She quoted the words of Lady Jersey 'Put not this additional burden upon us.' Women were not equal to men in endurance or nervous energy, and, she thought she might say, on the whole, in intellect.

Part of a report published in the *East Grinstead Observer* on 27 May 1911

Enquiry source 4F

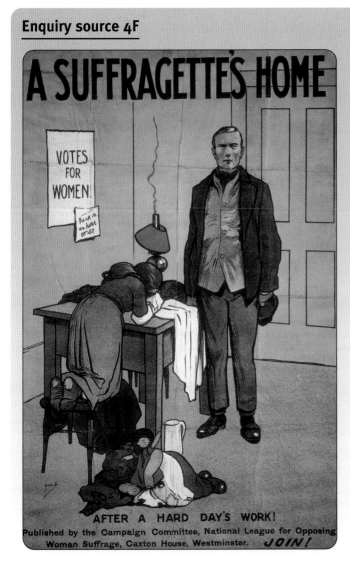

6.9 A poster designed by John Hassall in 1912 for the National League for Opposing Women's Suffrage

Enquiry source 4G

Until the suffragists fanned it into life, Anti-Suffragism had no cause or rationale, and without the stimulus provided by the steady conversion of politicians to the women's cause, not to mention the 'outrages' committed by Edwardian suffragettes, they would have found great difficulty in sustaining a campaign at all. In some sense, then, the Antis offer a barometer of the fluctuating fortunes of suffragism. They themselves appear to have appreciated the complexity of their relationship with their opponents; tactless speeches by male Antis aroused the sense of grievance among inactive women, while the more female Antis became drawn into active campaigning, the more they demonstrated that women were, after all, capable of playing a role in politics. Their peculiar aim, therefore, was somehow to quell the suffragist campaign and retire from public life before anyone had realised how effective they had been!

From Martin Pugh *The March of the Women* published in 2000

Question

Study Sources 4C, 4D and 4E.

How far are the views expressed in Source 4E supported by Sources 4C and 4D?

PRACTICE SOURCE EVALUATION

- Source 4A is a secondary source. What impressions does the author give of the nature of the anti-suffrage campaigns? What evidence is he likely to have found that enabled him to give these impressions? Are there any sources in this particular enquiry, or in this unit or Unit 5, which he might have used?
- Now ask the same questions of the other secondary source, 4G.
- Given what has been said in Source 4A about the anti-suffrage campaign, does Source 4B surprise you?
- What are the differences in message between the two visual sources, Source 4B and Source 4F?
- What are the points of agreement between Sources 4C and 4D?

SKILLS BUILDER

Study Sources 4E, 4F and 4G and use your own knowledge.

To what extent do you agree with the view expressed in Source 4G about the impact of the anti-suffragist campaign?

Unit summary

What have you learned in this unit?

The first decade of the twentieth century was marked in many ways by delay and frustration insofar as the enfranchisement of women was concerned. No one party or group gave wholehearted backing to the campaigns to give women the vote. The increasingly militant actions of the suffragettes confirmed some in their belief that women were not fit to be given the vote. For some, militancy was a distraction from the serious business of negotiating female enfranchisement and yet for others it was the only way of forcing votes for women onto the government's agenda. The government, for its part, responded to militancy with repression on an unprecedented scale and to the attempts at peaceful compromise, via the conciliation bills, with procrastination and duplicity. Nevertheless, a great deal of ground had been prepared and most thinking people were well aware that, sooner or later, women would have the right to vote.

What skills have you used in this unit?

You will have worked with the sources and, through their evaluation, have developed an understanding that things are not always as they seem! Politicians, for example, may say one thing in private and another in public; attitudes of politicians may change when they see an electoral advantage for their party; sometimes the media allow the attitudes of their readership to dictate their attitudes, and the public is a fickle beast. On the other hand, you will have remembered that some people remained true to their principles, no matter how buffeted by events. You will have cross-referenced to the activities of the WSPU, as described and analysed in Unit 5.

SKILLS BUILDER

1 Look back over this unit and Unit 5. Identify the sources that were generated by the media. How far is it possible to draw a conclusion about the attitude of the press to women's suffrage?

2 Who, or what, do you blame for the failure to enfranchise women by 1913? Work in pairs or small groups. Compare your views with those of other students. How have you used the evidence to back your views? Can you reach a class consensus about where blame lay?

3 To what extent do you think the WSPU scored an 'own goal' by resorting to militancy, thus 'proving' that they were unfit to be given the vote?

Exam tips

This is the sort of question you will find appearing on the examination paper as a (b) question.

4 Study Sources F, M and U and use your own knowledge.

Do you agree with the view, expressed in Source U, that the confrontation between the government and the suffrage campaigners was not 'wholly barren of results'?

You tackled (b) style questions at the end of Units 2 and 4. Look back to the exam tips you were given there because you will need to use them in order to answer this question. At the end of Unit 4 you created a spider diagram as a plan. This time, use whichever sort of plan you like best and which works for you. But be sure to plan!

- Be very sure you know what **view** is being expressed in Source U.
- **Analyse** and **interpret** Sources F and M so as to establish points that **support** and **challenge** the view given in Source U.
- **Cross-reference** between the sources by focusing on support and challenge.
- Use your **wider knowledge** both to reinforce and to challenge the points derived from the sources.
- Combine the points into **arguments** for and against the view given in Source U.
- **Evaluate** the conflicting arguments by considering the **quality of the evidence** used, involving a consideration of provenance (where appropriate) and the weight of evidence and range of supporting knowledge you can find in support.
- Present a **supported judgement** as to the validity of the stated view and/or any alternatives.

RESEARCH TASK

A local study

There were NUWSS and WSPU branches throughout Britain, as you can see from the map on page 68. Research your nearest local branches and find out what impact the suffrage campaigns had in your area.

7 1914 to 1928: a changed political landscape?

What is this unit about?

This unit focuses on the achievement of women's suffrage, partially in 1918 and fully in 1928. It explores the reasons why suffrage was finally granted and why it was granted in two stages, and in particular considers the role of the First World War as an agent of change. The impact of the 1918 Representation of the People Act on politics in the 1920s is considered, as are the reasons for the 1928 Equal Franchise Act.

Key questions

- Why were women enfranchised after the First World War?
- How did the enfranchisement of some women impact on politics in the 1920s?

Timeline

1914	August: Britain declares war on Germany WSPU suspends militancy
1915	coalition government set up
1916	David Lloyd George becomes Prime Minister Speaker's Conference set up
1918	February: Representation of the People Act gives the vote to women over the age of thirty Constance Markiewicz elected to parliament
1919	Nancy Astor becomes first woman MP to take her seat November: war ends Sex Disqualification Act
1920	Married Women's Property Act extended to Scotland
1922	Married Women's Maintenance Act Infanticide Act
1923	Matrimonial Causes Act
1925	Guardianship of Infants Act Bastardy Act The Widows, Orphans and Old Age Contributory Pensions Act
1928	Equal Franchise Act

Source A

7.1 A popular poster, published around 1912, which was later made into an even more popular postcard. It was designed by the Suffrage Atelier, an organisation aimed at encouraging artists to support the Women's Movement, and particularly the fight for the vote.

By the time war broke out in August 1914, women could be all of the people depicted in the top line of Figure 7.1, and yet be forbidden to vote in general elections. Men could display all of the characteristics depicted in the bottom line, and yet be permitted to vote in general elections. The logic of this was being increasingly challenged, and no more so than during the First World War.

SKILLS BUILDER

How far did this poster challenge the nineteenth-century philosophy of 'separate spheres'?

How did the different suffrage societies react to the outbreak of war in 1914?

War was declared on 4 August; six days later the Home Secretary, Reginald McKenna, released from prison all trade unionists who had been convicted of taking part in violent strikes and all suffragettes who had been imprisoned for acts of criminal militancy. Everyone's energies had to be focused on the war effort. McKenna made this gesture of good faith without any strings. No undertakings were required from the released prisoners, McKenna simply stating that he hoped they would 'respond to the feelings of their countrymen and countrywomen in this time of emergency'. And did the women do this?

What was the reaction of the WSPU to the war?

Source B

We believe that under the joint rule of enfranchised women and men, the nations of the world will, owing to women's influence and authority, find a way of reconciling the claims of peace and honour, and of regulating international relations without bloodshed. We nonetheless believe also that matters having come to the present pass it was inevitable that Great Britain should take part in the war and with that patriotism which has nerved women to endure torture in prison cells for the national good, we ardently desire that our country should be victorious – this because we hold that the existence of small nationalities is at stake, and that the status of Great Britain and France is involved.

It will be the future task of women, and only they can perform it, to ensure that the present world tragedy and the peril in which it places civilization, shall not be repeated and therefore, the WSPU will at the first possible moment step forward into the political arena in order to compel the enactment of a measure giving votes to women on the same terms as men.

From Emmeline Pankhurst's Circular Letter written on 13 August 1914

SKILLS BUILDER

How does Emmeline Pankhurst link the aims of the WSPU with the war effort?

Source C

Our position with regard to women fighting is this. If we are needed in the fighting line, we shall be there. If we are needed to attend to the economic prosperity of the country, we shall be there. What it is best in the interests of the state to do, women will do. But it must be clearly understood that if women do not actually take part in the fighting, that argues no inferiority, that argues no diminution of their claim to political equality. It simply means that men and women in co-operation decide the task which, in the interests of the whole, it is most necessary that they shall do. You must remember that if the men fight, the women are the mothers. Without the mothers you have no nation to defend. Therefore, we never had admitted – we never shall admit – that even though we do not take part in the actual fighting, we are not equally important in terms of citizenship. It is well known that you cannot maintain more than a certain proportion of your citizens in the fighting line. For everyone who fights you must have a number of non-combatants to feed him, to clothe him and to prevent the State for which he is fighting from crumbling into ruins. One thing is certain. You are not now utilising to the full the activities of women.

From a speech made by Christabel Pankhurst in the London Opera House on 8 September 1914 to her supporters

Questions

- What does Christabel envisage being women's contribution to the war?
- What do you think she most fears?

The WSPU threw itself into a vigorous patriotic campaign, placing its organisation and funds at the disposal of the government. Old enmities were set aside, and government and WSPU joined forces to fight side by side in a common cause. By 1915 two million men had gone abroad to fight and the government was desperate to recruit women workers. David Lloyd George, now Minister of Munitions, supplied the money and Emmeline Pankhurst the organisation and together they mounted a series of huge demonstrations and numerous smaller scale meetings that were designed to encourage women to join the workforce.

Source D

7.2 A photograph of part of the Women's Right to Serve march in London, July 1915. Lloyd George gave Emmeline Pankhurst £2,000 to stage this rally.

Question

Are you surprised that Emmeline Pankhurst and Lloyd George should be working so closely together?

The WSPU turned itself, almost overnight, into an intensely patriotic organisation. Members:

- called for women to be conscripted into the 'industrial' services;
- called for men to be conscripted into the armed services;
- urged the abolition of trade unions;
- gave white feathers to young men of military age whom they spotted wearing civilian clothes (a white feather was a sign of cowardice);
- believed **conscientious objectors** should be **interned**;
- in 1915 renamed their paper *Britannia* to demonstrate support for the Empire;
- launched a campaign directed at Russian women to encourage them to keep their men fighting;

Definitions

Conscientious objectors

People whose consciences would not let them fight.

Interned

Imprisoned without trial.

- toured the USA and Canada, lecturing on the need for women to become involved in the conflict.

What was the reaction of the East London Federation of Suffragettes to the war?

In January 1914, Christabel Pankhurst summarily expelled the ELFS from the WSPU (see page 65), but that wasn't the end of the ELFS, as Sylvia Pankhurst continued her social work among the poor in the East End of London. They:

- set up five centres, offering free milk and advice from a nurse to mothers and their babies;
- converted a pub, the Gunmaker's Arms, into a nursery and renamed it the Mother's Arms;
- opened a restaurant selling meals at 2d each, well below the current market price, even for the East End;
- argued for the control of food prices and profits;
- sent petitions to the government regarding the pay and working conditions of female munitions workers;
- unsuccessfully campaigned against Regulation 40D which made it a crime for a woman with a sexually transmitted disease to have sexual intercourse with a member of the armed forces. Look back to Josephine Butler and her fight to have the Contagious Diseases Act repealed (page 23) to remind yourself why this defeat was particularly important;
- campaigned for increases in the allowances paid to women whose husbands were away fighting;
- opened an unemployment bureau;
- established a toy and boot factory to help the unemployed.

However, not all Sylvia's work was focused on the poor and needy in the East End of London. In many ways she became revolutionary. She condemned the war, supported conscientious objectors and, sticking to her socialist principles, became one of Britain's leading anti-war agitators. Following Sylvia's developing socialist conscience, the ELFS changed its name firstly, in 1916 to the Workers' Suffrage Federation and finally, in 1918 to the Workers' Socialist Federation. Their newspaper changed, too, from *The Women's Dreadnought* to *The Workers' Dreadnought*.

What was the reaction of the National Union of Women's Suffrage Societies to the war?

Most members of the NUWSS viewed the prospect of war as an utter disaster. Trying to restore peace and order to Europe, members participated in a women's peace rally on 4 August 1914 that was organised by the Women's Labour League and the Women's Co-operative Guild. The intention of the rally was to urge Britain to adopt a neutral role as the storm clouds gathered, but by the time the rally was ending, Germany had invaded Belgium and war seemed inevitable. The women at the meeting were convinced they were facing a situation dominated by an inherent male preference for solving disputes by resorting to violence. Desperately, delegates passed a motion urging neutral nations to mediate and bring about an end to conflict. The press portrayed the meeting as unpatriotic and yet another sign of women's inability to understand politics. The following day, Lord Robert Cecil wrote to Millicent Fawcett expressing alarm. He was one of the Conservative Party's most influential supporters of women's suffrage.

Source E

Permit me to express my great regret that you should have thought it right not only to take part in the 'peace' meeting last night but also to have allowed the organisation of the National Union [the NUWSS] to be used for its promotion. Actions of that kind will undoubtedly make it very difficult for the friends of Women's Suffrage in both the Conservative and Liberal parties.

Even to me the action seems so unreasonable under the circumstances as to shake my belief in the fitness of women to deal with the great territorial questions and I can only console myself by the belief that in this matter the National Union do not represent the opinions of their fellow-countrywomen.

Part of a letter from Lord Robert Cecil to Millicent Fawcett written on 5 August 1914

Millicent Fawcett took the only possible course of action, choosing to follow a path that would more certainly lead to women's suffrage rather than a peace policy based on the dubious proposition that men were inherently violent. This split the NUWSS. Millicent Fawcett and her followers argued that the war effort had to be supported because a German victory would put back the cause of women's suffrage; those supporting a peace policy argued that women should assert the spiritual over physical force and urged a cessation of fighting and a negotiated peace. Matters came to a head in February 1915 at the NUWSS's annual council meeting and the ensuing row resulted in those supporting a peace policy leaving to form the Women's International League for Peace and Freedom.

Members of the NUWSS who remained:

- opened a register of voluntary workers who would find work for the unemployed;
- undertook relief work among the unemployed in cities and towns;
- set up a Women's Service Bureau in London to work with Belgian refugees and various war relief case study committees;
- established an employment register for women (by September 1914 over 44 per cent of women previously in employment were out of work) and interviewed women, placing them in jobs vacated by men who had left to fight;

Question

How reasonable do you find Lord Cecil's attitude? Discuss this in your group.

Definitions

TB (Tuberculosis)

A deadly and infectious disease commonly affecting the lungs. Such was the serious and widespread nature of the disease it is estimated to have been responsible for one third of all deaths in the early nineteenth century.

Women's Land Army

The Women's Land Army was established by the government in order to persuade women to work in agriculture. This was necessary because of the large numbers of farm labourers who had enlisted in the armed forces, and because of the need for Britain to become more self-sufficient in terms of foodstuffs. By 1917 there were over 260,000 women working as farm labourers.

- funded and set up Scottish Women's Hospitals Units that employed all-female teams of doctors, nurses and ambulance drivers and sent them into the war zones;

- provided medical relief to civilian populations in war-torn Europe, setting up maternity, **TB** and children's hospitals where they were needed.

Most importantly, the NUWSS retained its organisational structure, using it to deliver relief and support services. But this did mean that it could easily be swung into action should it be appropriate to resume the battle for women's suffrage.

How important was women's war work in gaining the franchise for women?

Unprecedented numbers of women worked during the war – and worked in occupations never before considered suitable for women. Immediately after the war, a limited number of women were given the vote. It is tempting to see the war as the vehicle of change. But was it? For over fifty years the male-dominated parliament had stubbornly resisted female enfranchisement. But by the end of the war, politicians appeared to have changed their minds. Why?

What work did women do?

Women from all social classes were involved in war work. Whether they were aristocratic women advising the government on health and employment, middle-class women joining the **Women's Land Army** or running voluntary organisations, working-class women taking over their husband's job for the duration of the war or young women leaving domestic service and working in munitions factories, women were there and were obviously doing the job.

Source F

7.3 The Women's Army Auxiliary Corps was established early in 1917 as the result of a decision taken by the Army Council to employ women in the Lines of Communication in France. In this photograph, WAAC drivers are maintaining the engine of an army officer's car at Abbéville, France, on 15 September 1917. Many WAACs served in the Advanced Mechanical Transport Depot in Abbéville. They kept hundreds of officers' cars on the road, servicing and driving them as well as keeping up with all the paperwork.

Source G

7.4 A photograph of women working in a munitions factory, making bullets, in May 1915. The friendliness of such places, and the high wages (£3–£5 a week compared to £18 a year as a domestic servant) made this sort of work attractive. However, munitions factories were dangerous places. Girls involved in putting TNT into shells were particularly at risk. Their hands and faces turned yellow – they were nicknamed 'canaries' – and they were only kept on the TNT work for a fortnight before being moved to other duties. The government was particularly concerned about the health and welfare of munitions workers.

Source H

7.5 This photograph shows women navvies pushing loaded wheelbarrows in Coventry during World War I, c.1917

But was it this work that changed the minds of politicians?

Question

Does anything about the photographs in Sources F, G and H surprise you?

What was the significance of the Speaker's Conference 1916?

It was generally accepted among politicians that there was a need to reform the franchise. The existing franchise law gave the vote to male householders who had occupied a dwelling for at least a year prior to an election. This meant that large numbers of men in the armed forces couldn't vote because they had been away from home for more than a year. Clearly this wasn't right. Men risking their lives for their country had to be allowed to vote. And a significant number of men, fighting for their country in horrendous circumstances, wouldn't have had the vote anyway because they were not householders. Something had to be done. To this end, an all-party conference, known as the Speaker's Conference, met behind closed doors in 1916 to discuss franchise reform.

Decisions and concerns

The feeling that all adult men should have the right to vote was overwhelming. And women too? This was a real step in the dark. Although it was clear that women had to be given the vote, it was far from clear which women and on what terms. After weeks of discussion and consultation, when the Speaker's Conference submitted its report to parliament, it recommended that 'some measure of woman suffrage should be conferred' on 'women who have attained a certain age', suggesting thirty or thirty-five as being appropriate.

Question

What was the problem with the Speaker's Conference proposals?

Source I

Sir John Simon and Mr Dickinson both considered there was a good chance of the Speaker's Conference recommending Women's Suffrage. The difficulty and danger would arise when concrete proposals for women's suffrage came to be discussed. The two members of parliament thought there was little or no chance of adult suffrage being recommended by the Conference and that for the Adultists* to press for it would risk the loss of even a general recommendation for women's suffrage in any form. A good deal of talk took place about various ways of dealing with the excess of women over men. Finally I think there was general agreement that raising the voting age for women was the least objectionable way of reducing the number of women.

Part of a memorandum of a conversation between Sir John Simon, the NUWSS's spokesman at the Speaker's Conference, and Millicent Fawcett on 15 December 1916

* Those who wanted adult suffrage for men and women on equal terms.

Source J

I hope you will not let the WS [Women's Suffrage societies] rush to the conclusion that our Conference has done nothing for the cause. I think that when the recommendations appear you will find that you have something very substantial. Only please do all you can to induce women to see that it will be bad tactics to fall foul of the conference because it may not have done all that they expected. The whole matter will need the most careful handling so as to avoid the risk of the Government having an excuse for saying, that as it is impossible to satisfy the advocates of women's suffrage, they will refrain from dealing with women's suffrage at all.

Part of a letter from W.H. Dickinson, a supporter of women's suffrage and member of the Speaker's Conference, to Millicent Fawcett, written on 19 January 1917

Source K

Mrs Rathbone thought that the Speaker's Conference recommendations were not at all satisfactory as such a franchise would be of no use to the female factory worker. We had been pressing for the franchise on account of the industrial dislocation to be expected after the war. She thought we might have to yield to it, but it seemed like throwing over the female factory worker altogether.

Mrs Strachey thought that the basis was thoroughly unsatisfactory, but that as it had been accepted by the Speaker's Conference, there was a strong presumption that it would be accepted by the House. We stand a chance of really getting something now, and opposition to it, based on however good reasons, might wreck the chance altogether.

From the Minutes of a meeting of the Executive Committee of the NUWSS on 1 February 1917

Source L

Millicent Fawcett: I think I may say that we shall be very gratified if the Prime Minister should see his way to improve, in a democratic direction, upon the recommendations of the Conference – but only so far as is consistent with the safety of the whole scheme. We should greatly prefer an imperfect scheme that can pass, to the most perfect scheme in the world that could not pass.

Mary Macarthur: Women munitions workers have asked me to say on their behalf that they do not ask for the vote as a reward for wartime services rendered. They ask it because they want to play their part in the great reconstruction work that is lying ahead of us all. We know there is no class which will be more affected by reconstruction proposals than the women who have come into industry during this emergency. We feel bound to point out to you that the proposals of the Speaker's Conference shut the door on the vast majority of women engaged on munitions work.

From an official record of the meeting between members of the NUWSS and the Prime Minister, David Lloyd George, on 29 March 1917

Why did politicians seem to change their minds about enfranchising women?

The recommendations of the Speaker's Conference summed up the views of its members; there was no minority report. As it turned out, the recommendations found favour with the House of Commons – the House of Commons that for over sixty years had set its face against giving women the vote. So what had happened to change the collective mind of the Commons?

- The fear that the enfranchisement of women would benefit one political party over another had largely vanished. Liberal and Labour politicians felt that the social mix of such a large group of women would not lead them necessarily to vote Conservative; Conservatives believed that most women over the age of 30 were likely to be moderate in their voting habits and so they had nothing to lose by agreeing to their enfranchisement.

- In 1915 the Liberal government was replaced by a coalition government, and so there was a greater likelihood of cross-party agreement to any decision to enfranchise women.

Question

Why were NUWSS members struggling with the Speaker's Conference proposals?

- In December 1916 David Lloyd George, a sympathiser, replaced the antagonistic Herbert Asquith as Prime Minister.

- The government itself, by 1916–17, contained many more MPs who were sympathetic to the cause. Andrew Bonar Law and Arthur Henderson were promoted to the Cabinet, replacing men who were opposed to votes for women.

- The cessation of WSPU militancy, for the duration of the war, and the universally acknowledged important contribution of women to the war effort, enabled many MPs to change their minds without loss of face.

- The international scene was changing. As the House of Commons, in 1918, debated votes for women, the House of Representatives in the USA was doing just the same and carried votes for women by a two-thirds majority; Australia, Canada (except Quebec), Denmark, Finland, Norway and New Zealand had already enfranchised women.

Source M

(1) Why, and in what sense, the House may ask, have I changed my views? My opposition to women suffrage has always been based on considerations of public expediency. I think that some years ago I ventured to use the expression 'Let the women work out their own salvation.' Well, Sir, they have. How could we have carried on the War without women? There is hardly a service in which women have not been at least as active as men, and wherever we turn we see them doing work which three years ago would have been regarded as falling exclusively within the province of men. But what moves me more in this matter is the problem of reconstruction once the War is over. The questions which will arise with regard to women's labour and women's functions are questions in which I find it impossible to withhold from women the right of making their voices heard. And let me add that, since the War began, we have had no recurrence of that detestable campaign which disfigured the annals of political agitation in this country, and no one can now contend that we are yielding to violence what we refused to concede to argument.

Part of a speech made by Herbert Asquith
to the House of Commons in 1917

(2) There are about fifteen thousand women on the [Electoral] Register – a dim, impenetrable lot, for the most part hopelessly ignorant of politics, credulous to the last degree, and flickering with gusts of sentiment like a candle in the wind.

Part of a speech made by Herbert Asquith
in Paisley in 1920

Question

Was Asquith a hypocrite?

Achieving the vote – but not for everyone

At the end of the debate on the Representation of the People Bill (1918) 385 MPs voted for the clause supporting votes for women, with only 55 voting against. What would happen in the Lords, that bastion of male supremacy? In a word, nothing. Lord Curzon, President of the League for Opposing Woman Suffrage (see page 99) urged peers to abstain from voting if they could not support the bill. And so, on 6 February 1918, the Representation of the People Act became law. It gave the vote to all men over the age of twenty one, and to all women over the age of thirty who were on the local government register or who were married to men who were. This was essentially a very conservative measure, and this goes some way towards explaining why its passage through parliament was so relatively untroubled.

Despite wartime declarations of gratitude to munitions workers, few of them were able to vote after 1918 because most of them were under thirty years of age.

Educated, middle-class single women who were the backbone of the suffrage societies were unlikely to be enfranchised. Even if they were over the age of thirty they were most likely to be found living with their parents or in rented accommodation and so did not qualify as local government voters and so could not have the parliamentary franchise.

It has been estimated that about 22 per cent of all women aged 30+ were excluded from the franchise because of the requirement to be on the local government electoral roll – and thus be householders or married to a householder.

Women over the age of thirty were believed to be stable, probably married and with children and so less likely to support radical reforms and feminist measures. Indeed, about 83 per cent of the women enfranchised in 1918 were wives and mothers.

Nevertheless, 8,400,000 women did gain the vote after the 1918 legislation and they made up 39.6 per cent of the electorate.

Justifiable celebrations?

Suffrage societies held a huge, celebratory party in Queen's Hall in March 1918. William Blake's poem 'Jerusalem' was set to music and sung lustily by all present. Millicent Fawcett declared the granting of the vote to women to be the greatest moment of her life. Others were less euphoric. Many were aware that they had not achieved equal suffrage rights for which they had been campaigning since the 1860s. Their legal status was still inferior to that of men. The battle was far from over.

Source N

AT LAST

7.6 A cartoon
published in the
magazine *Punch*
in 1918

SKILLS BUILDER

1 Was *Punch* being too triumphant?

2 Study all the *Punch* cartoons in this book. Has *Punch* displayed a consistent attitude to women's rights?

Source O

The manner in which the situation was exploited owed much to the experience the women's leaders had derived from the pre-war suffrage movements; it is also true that before the war the doors to a number of professions were already opening. Yet it is difficult to see how women could have achieved so much in anything like a similar time-span without the unique circumstances arising from the war.

From Arthur Marwick *The Deluge: British Society and the First World War* published in 1965

Source P

Whether the war influenced the debate about votes for women is rather doubtful. The role played by young women in munitions factories and other formerly male employment generated excellent copy for the newspapers. But it did not lead men generally to change their ideas about gender roles. The press, the government, the unions, and employers largely agreed in regarding women's war work as temporary. On the contrary, the war made them see women's traditional roles as wives and mothers as even more important, now that the flower of British manhood was being frittered away in Flanders. But if the war had little impact on the decision to give women the vote, it did almost certainly help to influence the form that enfranchisement took in that it strengthened the feeling that the vote should not be a reward for single women so much as a recognition of married women.

From Martin Pugh *The March of the Women* published in 2000

How far was the political landscape changed in the 1920s?

Source Q

The Representation of the People Act had not been on the statute book a fortnight before the House of Commons discovered that every bill which came before it had a 'woman's side', and the Party whips began eagerly to ask 'what the women thought'. The precincts of the House of Commons, which had been firmly closed to all women since the early days of militant agitation, were now opened, and access to members became wonderfully easy. Letters from women constituents no longer went straight into wastepaper baskets but received elaborate answers, and the agents of the women's societies were positively welcomed at Westminster.

From Ray Strachey *The Cause: A Short History of the Women's Movement in Britain* published in 1928. She was a member of the NUWSS and its parliamentary secretary 1916–21, throughout the crucial years of negotiation prior to the 1918 Representation of the People Act.

Was Ray Strachey being over-optimistic? The political advances of women in the 1920s were dependent upon the willingness of the political parties to accommodate them. The right to vote and a handful of women MPs were not very likely to change the male mind-set in parliament.

Did women flock to become MPs?

Seven women candidates stood for election to the House of Commons in 1918, but only one of them, Constance Gore-Booth (who became the Countess Markiewicz after her marriage to a Polish count), was successful. However, she had an alternative agenda. A strong advocate of Irish nationalism, she refused to take her seat because she did not recognise the legitimacy of Westminster to legislate for Ireland. She, and the other Sinn Féin candidates, set up their own parliament, the Dail Éireann, in Dublin in 1919.

The first woman to be elected to parliament in her own right was Nancy Astor, who took over her husband's constituency in Plymouth when he moved to the House of Lords. Over the next ten years, the number of women MPs gradually increased: in 1922 there were five women MPs and by 1929 their numbers had swollen to fourteen. Even so, they were heavily outnumbered by the 601 male MPs. It was in 1929 that Margaret Bondfield, became the first female member of the Cabinet, serving as the Minister of Labour in the second Labour government until 1931. Parliament, needless to say, wasn't physically ready for women. In 1922 the five women MPs had to share an office and there was no women's lavatory in the building.

What was the likelihood of an all-women's party being established?

Christabel Pankhurst tried to start an exclusively female political party, and, with so many women's suffrage organisations in existence, this didn't seem to be an unreasonable ambition on her part. Historian Annette Mayer explains why this didn't happen.

Source R

This expectation did not materialise as women MPs were rapidly subsumed into the intricacies of party politics. Party loyalty, especially within the Labour Party, was considered to be of higher priority than the interests of one faction. Such demands presented many women MPs with an unwelcome dilemma. The danger would be that without active promotion of women's issues, these important questions would remain in the background. Yet if they neglected the overall party's interests or, indeed, the concerns of their male constituents it would not be a good personal recommendation when they stood for re-election. Ultimately, therefore, women's political futures rested within the mainstream parties. What mattered was the reception accorded to women by Labour and the Conservatives.

From Annette Mayer *Women in Britain 1900–2000* published in 2002

How welcoming was the Labour Party?

In 1918 the Labour Party published a new constitution, making 'women' one of several affiliated groups, which included trade unions, socialist societies and local labour parties. Women's sections were set up, enabling four women to be elected to Labour's National Executive. Women within the Labour Party faced a dilemma. Labour's main objective was to remove inequalities in society and repeal old, and refuse to support new, discriminatory legislation. So far, so good. Or was it? Labour women would hardly oppose measures directed at achieving, say, equality, in the workplace. But too often these policies and bills were directed at the rights of the working man, not the working women. Unemployment rose after the First World War, and trade union members understandably wanted to protect the interests of their (mainly) male members. Too often women employees were the first to be sacrificed in the effort to protect men's jobs (see pages 166–8). However, the appointment of Dr Marion Philips as chief woman organiser with the responsibility of increasing the number of female voters, does show something of the commitment of Labour to the female vote.

How welcoming was the Conservative Party?

Accepting that female enfranchisement was going to happen, the Conservative Party appreciated the advantages to it of limiting the franchise to defined groups of the over-thirties. These were the more stable, married women – probably mothers – who, they argued to themselves, would be likely to vote Conservative. The women's section of the Primrose League and the all-female Women's Unionist Organisation were affiliated to the Conservative Party and formed an effective force within the party as a whole. Middle-class educated women, with time on their hands, were well able to work voluntarily in the fields of administration and fundraising, resulting in a solid core of support for the domestic policies of Conservative governments.

Levelling the playing field

After the enfranchisement of women, a number of other reforms were implemented by successive governments, aimed at ironing out some of the more glaring inequalities:

- 1919 Sex Disqualification (Removal) Act gave women the right to become jurors, magistrates and barristers, and to enter the higher ranks of the civil service. It also removed legal barriers to women becoming graduates of Oxford and Cambridge universities.
- 1922 Married Women's Maintenance Act allowed women 40 shillings for herself and 10 shillings for each child.
- 1922 Infanticide Act removed the charge of murder from mothers who killed their infant children, thus recognising that some women were medically depressed after giving birth.
- 1923 Matrimonial Causes Act allowed women to divorce on the same grounds as men.
- 1923 Bastardy Act increased maintenance payments to single mothers.
- 1925 Guardianship of Infants Act gave mothers the same custody rights as fathers.
- 1925 Widows, Orphans and Old Age Contributory Pensions Act provided a pension for widows of insured men
- 1928 Equal Franchise Act gave the vote to men and women on equal terms.

To what extent did parliamentary politics change?

The nature of parliamentary politics did not change at all. Suffragists hoped that women's gentler, less confrontational approach would feminise parliament. Not a bit of it. The House of Commons remained essentially a man's institution, programmed to deal with matters of importance in a masculine way. After all, men dominated the membership. Women simply adapted, as women always have done down the ages. They learned adversarial debate and they sided on domestic issues along party, not feminist, lines.

Equal franchise: the final push?

After 1918, women were still unequal and millions of them still disenfranchised. The final push had to come with franchise equality. In 1918 the coalition government's manifesto undertook to remove inequalities between men and women. Yet no government bill sought to do this. The Labour Party had consistently supported equal franchise, yet when it was briefly in power in 1924, it resisted all attempts to introduce an equal franchise bill. This was such a familiar story. Politicians gave lip service to principle, but when it came to putting principles into action, they drew back because they were afraid of the outcome. But equal franchise did come about – and only ten years after the limited franchise granted in 1918. And in the end it was granted by a Conservative government.

Read through the next four sources and work out why this happened.

Source S

There is undoubtedly a growing feeling [among Conservative women] that if the government do not see their way to appointing the Conference [on franchise reform] or to appointing it in such time as will allow of its finding becoming operative at the next election, it will do us a lot of harm when that time comes.

There is no question of the merits of the case being involved and the opinion of Unionist [Conservative] women differs widely on the subject, but even among those who differ there seems to be a measure of agreement that a promise has been made that the subject shall be dealt with, and that it will be very disastrous if the Prime Minister can be represented at the Election as not having redeemed a Pledge.

We depend at elections upon masses of women with few really definite convictions, whose instincts are in the main naturally conservative but who might easily be swept away if their faith in the sanctity of the Prime Minister's pledges were shaken by skilful manoeuvres on the part of the enemy.

Part of a letter from Lady Gwendolen Elveden to Colonel F.S. Jackson,
Conservative Party Chairman, written on 16 November 1926

Source T

It has become increasingly clear, election after election, that the woman who was enfranchised in 1918 was either the married woman or the woman of property. The situation thus became clear: it was the woman occupied in industry and in the professions who by the terms of the 1918 measure were shut out from its advantages. It has been estimated, indeed, that only about one in fifteen of the women wage earners have the right to vote. The great majority of women in industry leave before they are 30 to get married, while those over 30 in many cases live either with their families, or in furnished rooms, big hostels etc. It is a matter of common knowledge that comparatively few professional women are the proud possessors of houses, or even of unfurnished rooms of their own. The importance of this becomes manifest if we remember that almost every year parliament is discussing legislation dealing with the conditions of women workers. In certain the interests of women workers clash with those of men. It certainly cannot be right that the labour of adult women should be controlled by a parliament which is not responsible to those whose livelihood it is directing.

Part of an article 'The Equal Franchise' written by Eva Hubback and published in the journal *Fortnightly Review* in April 1928. In 1919 the NUWSS changed its name to the National Union of Societies for Equal Citizenship. In the 1920s, Eva Hubback was its secretary.

SKILLS BUILDER

For what different reasons did Lady Gwendolen Elvedon and Eva Hubback press for equal franchise?

Source U

At the Cabinet, Stanley [Baldwin] opened with a short résumé of the position with regard to our pledges on the women's vote concluding that the only thing we could do was to give it all round at 21. Winston [Churchill] led the opposition with great vehemence and our opinions were then taken all the way round. I took the view with many others that 25 for both sexes would be preferable but did not think we should see it through and therefore favoured 21. In the end 21 prevailed by a considerable majority. Winston very unhappy as, indeed were also FE [Smith, Lord Birkenhead] and several others.

An extract from the diary of Leo Amery written on 12 April 1927. In 1927, Leo Amery was the MP for Birmingham Sparkbrook and colonial secretary in the Conservative government.

Source V

The subjection of women, if there be such a thing, will not now depend on any creation of the law, nor can it be remedied by any action of the law. Women will have, with us, the fullest rights. The ground and justification for the old agitation is gone, and gone forever.

Part of Prime Minister Stanley Baldwin's speech in the House of Commons, in March 1928 during the debate on the Equal Franchise Bill

Definition

Parliamentary whips

Whips are the MPs who are appointed by party leaders to manage, and if necessary, discipline, MPs in their own political party. They can, for example, insist that party members vote in a particular way.

By the time the Representation of the People (Equal Franchise) Bill reached the Commons, the real struggle had happened beforehand. Introduced by the Conservative government, the bill was supported by both Liberal and Labour parties, and what opposition there was came from Conservative backbenchers. The vote (387 to 10) seemed like a complete triumph for supporters of the bill, but it masks frantic behind-the-scenes manoeuvring. Aware of the level of opposition, the government refused to allow a free vote and applied the **parliamentary whips**. Aware of the consequences of ignoring the whips, many Conservative MPs, including Winston Churchill, simply absented themselves on the day of the vote. The huge vote in favour of equal franchise must, too, reflect the actions of MPs who, realising that the passage of the bill was inevitable, did not want to be seen by the new women electors as opposing the female vote.

Source W

Opinions differ regarding the extent to which the woman's suffrage campaign was responsible for securing the 1928 Act. The political parties had vested interests in trying to attract the women's vote. Political expediency, therefore, has to be regarded as the major factor in persuading both Labour and Conservatives to cease their ambiguity towards reform and to give equal franchise their eventual assent. Yet how significant was the organised pressure from the suffrage societies? According to feminist historians, there was a considerable degree of continuity within the suffrage movement from pre-war to post-war campaigns. Although activism was less militant after 1918, suffrage societies had maintained a co-ordinated and law-abiding campaign with pressure applied regularly on politicians.

From Annette Mayer *Women in Britain 1900–2000* published in 2002

Source X

7.7 'Free and Independent', a *Punch* cartoon used as the front cover of *The Vote* published on 6 July 1928. The cartoon appeared in *Punch* on 27 June 1928.

SKILLS BUILDER

1 What point is the cartoonist making in Source X above?

2 Is he correct?

3 Why was the cartoon published twice, once by *Punch* and then on the front cover of *The Vote*?

Unit summary

What have you learned in this unit?

You have learned that after over sixty years of campaigning, of advances and setbacks, sacrifices and triumphs, women finally had the vote on the same terms as men. The various political parties, and parliament itself, had shown themselves to be more interested in political advantage than principle. The women suffragists had shown themselves to be ready to compromise and in doing so finally ended up with what they had sought for so long: equal franchise. But this was not the end. Those who believed the Act would ensure equality between men and women were to be sadly mistaken. The passing of the Representation of the People (Equal Franchise) Act simply opened the door by a crack, enabling those who supported the enfranchisement of women to begin to create pressure for greater legal and civil equality. It was to take a further fifty years for equal opportunities legislation to find its way onto the statute books.

What skills have you used in this unit?

You have evaluated source material in order to determine the reactions of various suffrage societies to the outbreak of war in 1914, and to the reactions of politicians. You will have understood that the reactions of individuals within the various societies did not necessarily mirror those of their leaders. You have used source material to explore the range of women's contributions to the war effort. You will have considered and evaluated the pressures on the government to include women in the Representation of the People Act of 1918 and understood the dilemma posed to the women's suffrage societies by the age and property restrictions suggested by the Speaker's Conference. Finally, you will have evaluated the reasons why universal suffrage was finally achieved in 1928.

SKILLS BUILDER

1   Look carefully at Sources F, G and H.

   For each photograph, work out how a woman doing that particular job might impact people's views as to whether women should be given the vote or not.

   Discuss this with a partner. Do you both have the same views – and for the same reasons?

2   Read both parts of Source M and use the index to look back to Asquith's earlier views on women's suffrage.

   Do you think Asquith genuinely had changed his mind on the subject of women's suffrage? Debate this – but remember to back your arguments with evidence.

3   Did the achievement of votes for women owe more to Emmeline Pankhurst or Millicent Fawcett?

Exam tips

This is the sort of question you will find appearing on the examination paper as a (b) question. This one, however, is slightly different in that you are asked to use only two sources with your own knowledge. You may be asked to use two sources and you may be asked to use three – so be prepared for either and don't be surprised! Remember, though, that if you choose a (b) question that asks you to use two sources, don't assume that this is an easier question than one that asks you to use three. The two sources will be 'meatier' and more complex than the three.

4 Study Sources O and P and use your own knowledge.

Do you agree with the view that some women were given the vote in 1918 because of women's contribution to the war effort?

- The **structure** of the question is different from the (b) questions you have worked on previously in the exam-style Questions. This time the 'view' isn't contained in one of the sources but is given in the question.
- You will see that the two sources (O and P) are much **denser** and **more complex** than sources you have dealt with previously. This means that they will need very careful reading.
- **Think carefully about** what each source says about why some women were given the vote in 1918, and jot this down. You will need to refer to these notes when you make your plan.

Now draw up your plan.

- **Analyse** Sources O and P for points that **support** and points that **challenge** the view that women were given the vote because of their contribution to the war effort.
- **Cross-reference** between the sources for points of **agreement** and **disagreement**.
- Use your **wider knowledge** both to reinforce and to challenge the points you have derived from the sources.
- Combine the points into an **argument** for or against the view given in the question.
- **Evaluate** the conflicting arguments by considering the **quality of the evidence used**.
- Reach a balanced, **supported conclusion**.

RESEARCH TASK

Emmeline Pankhurst and Millicent Fawcett

Too often, individuals are in the limelight for a specific event and then they vanish from sight.

Find out what happened to Emmeline Pankhurst and Millicent Fawcett in the years after 1918.

Once you have completed your research, answer this question: are you surprised at what happened to them?

8 Educating women and girls: the key to success?

What is this unit about?

This unit focuses on the education of girls and women in this period. It considers the changing educational opportunities open to them and the reasons why these opportunities changed and developed. The education of girls from poor families is addressed, as is that of girls from middle-class and wealthy homes. The opening of higher education to young women is considered. Changing attitudes to the education of girls and young women by the state, by men and by the girls and women themselves, permeate this enquiry.

Key questions

- How far had the education of women and girls improved during this period?
- To what extent did education overturn the 'separate spheres' philosophy?

Timeline

1850	Frances Mary Buss founded the North London Collegiate School for Ladies
1858	Dorothea Beale became principal of Cheltenham Ladies' College
1864	Schools Enquiry Commission set up to investigate the education of children from middle-class homes
1865	formation of the Kensington Society
1865	Elizabeth Garrett Anderson becomes first woman on the Medical Register
1869	first women's college at Cambridge University founded in Hitchin, moving to Girton in 1872
1870	Forster's Education Act introduced a dual system of education, whereby the state provided schools to fill gaps left by the voluntary sector
1871	Newnham College, Cambridge, founded
1876	Sandon's Act penalised parents who kept their children away from school Enabling Bill, authorising all medical corporations to admit women to their examinations
1880	Mundella's Act made education compulsory for children under the age of thirteen
1891	a government grant made education free in elementary schools
1892	St Hilda's College, Oxford, founded
1893	school leaving age fixed at eleven
1899	school leaving age raised to twelve

1902   Balfour's Act sets up local education authorities to take over the administration
        of education from school boards

1906   free school meals introduced for the children of the poor

1907   free medical inspections introduced for the children of the poor
        free places in secondary schools for the children of the poor

1918   Fisher's Act raised the school leaving age to fourteen

Source A

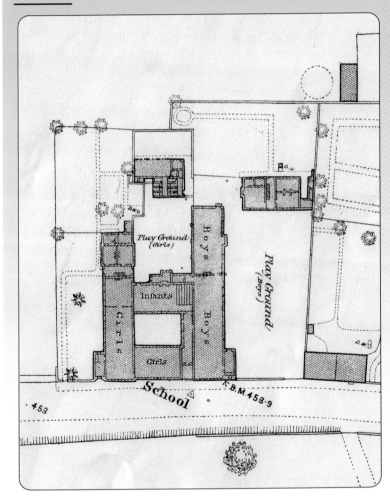

8.1 By 1870, the National Society for the Education of the Poor in the Principles of the Established Church controlled over 17,000 schools, all of which were called National Schools. This is the ground plan of one of these schools: the National School in Tring, Hertfordshire. It was drawn on a scale of 500 inches to 1 mile and published by Ordnance Survey in 1876.

SKILLS BUILDER

1   What does this school plan tell you about the education of boys and girls in Tring School at this time?

2   What tentative conclusions can you draw from this plan about attitudes towards the education of girls?

It was, of course, important to fight for the rights of women to vote in general elections and so have an input into the ways in which the country was governed. But if women were to play a full part in society they had to be enabled to enter the world of work – and enter it on the same terms as men. The key to this was education.

How important was legislation in providing education for working-class girls?

Definition

Dame school

A small primary school run mainly by women in their own homes.

Non-sectarian education

An education not based on religion or religious principles.

Before 1870, the Christian church was heavily involved in providing elementary education for working-class children. The non-conformist British and Foreign Schools Society and the Anglican National Society took the largest part and were in receipt of government grants for doing so. There were other schools, **dame schools** for example, that provided **non-sectarian education**, but these were by far in a minority. Education, however, was not compulsory and it was not free. It was therefore inevitable that girls from poor families lost out. When young, they were kept at home to help raise younger siblings; when old enough to earn a wage, they were usually sent into domestic service. Why, after all, did girls need to learn to read and write?

Times, though, were changing. The continuing population growth put enormous pressure and increasing strain on the ability of the voluntary sector to provide sufficient schools and teachers in the cities, towns and villages that wanted them, and there were increasingly large gaps in the provision they were able to make.

It was at this point that the Liberal MP for Bradford, West Yorkshire, W.E. Forster, put forward his education bill.

1870 Elementary Education Act (Forster's Act)

In Source B, W.E. Forster explains to the House of Commons why urgent action is necessary.

Source B

We must not delay. Upon the speedy provision of elementary education depends our industrial prosperity. It is of no use trying to give technical teaching to our artisans without elementary education; uneducated labourers – and many of our labourers are uneducated – are, for the most part, unskilled labourers, and if we leave our workfolk any longer unskilled, notwithstanding their strong sinews and determined energy, they will become over-matched in the competition of this world. Upon this speedy provision depends also, I fully believe, the good, the safe working of our constitutional system. To its honour, parliament has lately decided that England shall in future be governed by popular government. I am one of those who would not wait until the people were educated before I would trust them with political power. If we had thus waited we might have waited long for education, but now that we have given them political power we must not wait any longer to give them education.

Part of W.E. Forster's speech to MPs, from *Hansard* 17 February 1870

Source C

There shall be in every school district a sufficient amount of public elementary schools for all children.

Where there is an insufficient number of schools, a School Board shall be formed to supply such deficiency.

Every child attending a school shall pay fees prescribed by the School Board. The Board may remit part of such fee when they are of the opinion the child is unable to pay because of poverty.

If a School Board satisfies the Education Department that, on the grounds of poverty, it is expedient to provide a school at which no fees shall be required, the Board may provide such a school.

Any sum required to meet any deficiency in the school fund shall be paid out of the local rate.

Every School Board may make bye-laws (i) requiring the parents of children of such age, not less than five years nor more than thirteen years, to cause such children (unless here is some reasonable excuse) to attend school, provided that any such bye-law shall provide for the exemption of a child if one of Her Majesty's Inspectors certifies that such child has reached a standard of education specified in such bye-law.

From *Statutes of the Realm* (the 33rd and 34th Statute of Victoria) summarising some of the main clauses of Forster's Education Act, 1870

Questions

- What reasons does Forster give for needing to educate working-class children?
- There is no mention here of girls. How far could Forster's Education Act help in their education?

The underlying importance of the 1870 Act was that the state, having previously subsidised voluntary education, was now going to supplement it. Voluntary schools were not abolished; the state simply filled the gaps in the provision supplied by the voluntary sector (see Unit 3, pages 32–4). Overall, far more school places were provided: new state-funded schools were built, and the voluntary sector, in the spirit of competition, did likewise.

In 1880, Mundella's Act made attendance at school compulsory for children aged between five and ten, and, in 1891, education in elementary schools was free to all pupils as the result of a government grant. School Attendance Committees were set up to enforce these regulations and so, it was assumed, drive up literacy.

Questions

- Do these statistics prove that legislation was effective in raising literacy levels?
- How would you explain the consistently lower performances of girls when compared to that of boys?

Source D

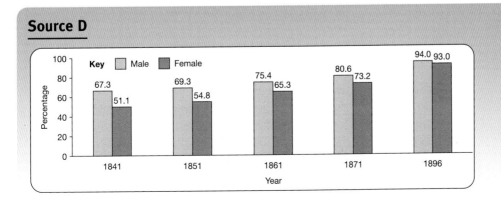

8.2 Rises in literacy level, 1841–96 from M. Sanderson *Education, Economic Change and Society in England 1780–1870* published in 1983

1902 Education Act (Balfour's Act)

Until this Act, full-time education beyond the elementary stage was open only to those parents (generally middle-class) who could afford the fees of grammar, private or public schools. Some school boards tried to provide some form of secondary and technical education, but they struggled because they were too small. Most working-class children, even the brightest, had little chance of continuing their education beyond elementary school.

This Education Act, introduced by the Conservative government led by Arthur Balfour (hence the name Balfour's Act) abolished the 2,568 school boards and set up 328 county council education authorities. These were large enough to build and maintain elementary and secondary schools.

It was always intended that secondary schools should charge fees, but in 1907 a significant change was made. Secondary schools receiving money from the public purse were instructed to make 25 per cent of their places available free of charge to clever children from elementary schools. In reality, only about one child in thirty from elementary schools won, by competitive written examinations, one of these scholarships. What was important, however, was that a ladder of opportunity had been created that would enable some of the poorest children to realise their full potential. The 'ladder' however, was a bit shaky. In 1930 only about one in eight children from an elementary school went to secondary schools, and one in 240 young people who started their education in an elementary school went to university. About 80 per cent of children attended the same school for their whole education, and most of these were girls.

How did the legislation of the Liberal governments of 1906–14 help children?

The Liberal Party that was swept to power in 1906 embarked on wave after wave of reforming legislation. Some of this legislation related to children (and therefore to girls) and because it concerned children's welfare, it had an indirect impact on their ability to learn.

- The 1906 Education (Provision of Meals) Act allowed local authorities to use public money to provide free meals for children of needy parents.

- Sir Robert Morant, the permanent secretary at the Board of Education (and therefore a civil servant) was determined to see medical provision introduced into the nation's schools. He managed to slip the relevant clauses into a complicated and technical piece of legislation and few MPs noticed or understood what he had done. Once the bill became law as the Education (Administrative Procedures) Act in 1907, Morant issued directives and circulars to local authorities, regulating the service and authorising them to provide treatment as well as inspection.

- The Children and Young Persons Act of 1908 brought together several older Acts, streamlining and extending their provisions. Specifically:

Question

Do you think it more likely that girls or boys would win scholarships to secondary schools?

- Children were made 'protected persons' which meant that their parents could be prosecuted for cruelty or neglect;
- Private children's homes were to be registered and inspected;
- Publicans were forbidden to allow children under the age of 14 into public houses;
- Shopkeepers were forbidden to sell cigarettes to children under fourteen years of age;
- Juvenile courts and remand homes were set up to separate children from adult offenders.

Question

- How would this legislation affect girls' learning?

What did girls learn at elementary school?

Girls learned, of course, the subjects they were taught. They also learned something far more subtle: their place in society.

Source E

The Department [of Education] issued Codes of precise regulations about the subjects which could be taught in schools and the grants payable for their instruction. Their range expanded over the period until, by 1895, there were 30 possible subjects. Leaving aside the complex regulations governing their teaching, it would be fair to say that what little effect this expansion had on girls was overwhelmingly that of differentiating their educational experience from that of boys even further. If taught additional subjects at all, the boys might study a variety including animal physiology, mechanics and algebra. For the girls, it was first theoretical domestic economy, and later cookery, laundry work and housewifery that occupied their time.

From Felicity Hunt (ed.) *Lessons for Life: The Schooling of Girls and Women 1850–1950* published in 1987

Source F

Elder sisters, you may work
Work and help your mothers
Darn the stockings, mend the shirts
Father's things, and brothers'.
Younger boys, and you may work
If you are but willing
Thro' the week in many ways
You may earn your shilling.

From Jarrold *New Code Reading Books II* published in 1871. A book used to teach reading in most elementary schools.

Source G

(i) Boys would miss just one morning or afternoon a week. Girls would miss two or three or four.

(ii) A girl seldom came to school more than eight times a week because she had to stay at home and help on washing day. This was perfectly acceptable to all concerned.

[There were ten possible attendances in a five-day week]

A. Davin in *'A centre of humanising influence': the schooling of working-class girls under the London School Board 1870–1902*, which was an unpublished paper written in 1978, reports what London teachers said about truancy

SKILLS BUILDER

What do Sources E, F and G tell you about the lessons girls learned about their place in society?

Source H

8.3 A science class c.1908

SKILLS BUILDER

To what extent does Source H give a different message from Sources E, F and G?

Source I

There was an enormous gulf between the intentions of those who promoted a sex-differentiated curriculum and aimed to ensure that every 14-year-old girl would be a skilled and resourceful housewife, and their achievements. Nevertheless, the ideology behind the curriculum was powerful, and provided school girls with an image of woman as servicing others. Schooling secured woman's imprisonment in domesticity.

From Annmarie Turnbull 'Learning Her Womanly Work: The Elementary School Curriculum 1870–1914' in Felicity Hunt (ed.) *Lessons for Life* published in 1987

How were the daughters of middle-class parents educated?

Most girls, until the mid-nineteenth century, were educated at home by governesses (see page 7) or, occasionally, sent to private schools. Girls had to be taught just enough of the basic subjects so that they could make good (but not too intelligent) conversation at their husband's dinner table, and accomplishments that would make them good wives: needlework and singing, French, sketching and painting, some croquet and tennis, and perhaps a little genteel (side-saddle) horse-riding. They learned by example how to receive visitors and the proper ways in which to make visits. They learned, too, the principles of running a household – how to manage the servants and possibly do domestic accounts. In short, the daughters of the middle classes were taught everything they needed to know for their future careers as wives.

Source J

(i) My mother advertised [for a governess] and hundreds of answers were received. She began by eliminating all those in which bad spelling occurred, next the wording and composition were criticised, and lastly a few of the writers were interviewed and a selection was made. But alas! An inspection was made of our exercise-books and revealed so many uncorrected faults, that a dismissal followed, and another search resulted in the same way. I can remember only one really clever and competent teacher; she had been educated in a good French school.

Having had no success at finding a suitable governess, Dorothea was sent to school.

(ii) It was a good school, considered much above average for sound instruction; our mistresses had taken pains to arrange various schemes of knowledge; yet what miserable teaching we had in many subjects; history was learned by committing to memory little manuals; rules of arithmetic were taught, but the principles were never explained. Instead of reading and learning the masterpieces of literature, we repeated week by week the 'Lamentations of King Hezekiah', and the pretty but somewhat weak 'Mother's Picture'.

Dorothea Beale, who was born in 1831, describes her education as a young girl

Enter Frances Mary Buss

On 4 April 1850 an entirely new and different school opened in Camden Town, London: the North London Collegiate School for Ladies. Starting with thirty-five girls, there were 115 by the end of the year; the school grew and grew in popularity and was to become the model for all future day schools for girls. What was the school for? And why was it so popular?

Source K

The deplorable ignorance of the poor, half a century ago, was a great national evil. Philosophers and statesmen have co-operated to diminish it. However, whilst their attention was directed to the poor man, they altogether forgot the tax and rate payer, the voter and that middle class of the community in whose hands our lives, our prosperity, nay, even our liberty depends.

Written by Frances Mary Buss in 1850

Question

Why was the North London Collegiate School established?

Source L

But while all these various institutions were being established for the education of Boys, it appears almost incredible that the lack of schools for Girls, which should provide them with a sound education, was entirely overlooked. Four years ago, an important step was taken by the establishing of Queen's College for Ladies in Harley Street. The flourishing state of Queen's College has proved the necessity for such an institution. However, an institution of this kind appeals to a wealthy class of Parents, the college expenses being too great to enable parents of limited means to bestow such an education upon all their girls if they form part of a large family. It is at this point that the benefit of the North London Collegiate School will be felt, where a liberal education and the accomplishments necessary for ladies can be obtained at a very moderate expense.

From the first Prize Day report of 1850 from the North London Collegiate School

Source M

The course of education will comprise the following subjects:

Religious instruction. Scripture, History and Geography. English Language and Literature. Elements of Latin. Writing and Arithmetic. French language and literature. Drawing, from models and nature. The Principles of Perspective. Singing upon the System of Mr John Hullah. The Leading Facts of Natural Philosophy and other branches of Science and Art. Plain and Ornamental Needlework.

Extras

The Italian and German languages. The Pianoforte. Harmony and Musical Composition. Solo Singing. Painting in Water colours. Dancing. By Qualified teachers, at a Moderate Additional Charge.

Terms:
- £2.2s per Quarter, payable in advance;
- books and stationery supplied at a moderate charge;
- hours of attendance from Ten to Three;
- the vacations will be a Week at Easter and Michaelmas, a month at Midsummer, and three weeks at Christmas;
- a large Garden will be appropriated to the Recreation of the Pupils.

From the North London Collegiate School prospectus, 1850

Question

What, in this prospectus, would alarm a father believing in the 'separate spheres' philosophy? What would reassure him?

Source N

8.4 A photograph of some of the girls who started school at the newly opened North London Collegiate School, taken by R.W. Buss, the father of Frances Mary Buss, in 1850

At the time girls were not allowed to sit public examinations (similar to modern-day GCSEs, A levels, Diplomas and BTecs) and **Frances Mary Buss** (see page 145) was determined to change this if girls' learning and achievement was to get the recognition it deserved. In 1863, following intense lobbying by herself and Emily Davies, the authorities allowed girls to sit the examinations – but unofficially. Fifteen girls from NLCS passed the examinations without any signs of the nervous exhaustion that they were supposed to suffer as a result of being exposed to such stress, and as a result of this experiment, in 1867 all such examinations were officially opened to girls throughout the country.

The school went from strength to strength. A sister school, Camden School, was opened in 1871 and by 1878, 894 girls were being educated with a further 140 on the waiting list. By this time the schools had changed their status from private schools to endowed schools. This meant that scholarships and reduced fees could be offered to clever girls from poorer families.

Question

Look back at the Balfour Education Act (page 132). Would poor parents of clever girls be more likely, do you think, to opt for the local authority schools or schools like the North London Collegiate and Camden School? Why?

And enter Dorothea Beale

Go back to **Dorothea Beale** (see page 133), the girl whose mother couldn't find her a suitable governess (Source J, see also page 145). She came from a privileged background and it was to a privileged school she went as headmistress and stayed for forty-eight years, turning Cheltenham Ladies' College into a prestigious boarding school for the daughters of the privileged. How did this happen? After a year as head teacher at the Clergy Daughters' School in Casterton, Cumbria she took time out to write her *Text Book of English and General History*. Meanwhile, events in Cheltenham were going to impact on the rest of her life.

Cheltenham College for Boys was founded in 1841 and was a flourishing and successful school. But it was, of course, for boys only. However, in 1853 the Principal, vice-Principal and four professional gentlemen in Cheltenham, having daughters of a similar age, were progressive enough to want them to have the same sort of education as the boys. They were determined to set up a similar school for girls. This they did, and in February 1854 Cheltenham Ladies' College opened with eighty-two girls and with Annie Proctor as their headmistress. After four years she resigned and the stage was set for Dorothea Beale to begin her life's work. By the time she died in 1906, the College had grown to accommodate some 1,000 pupils and had an international reputation.

Source O

The true meaning of the word education is not instruction. It is intellectual, moral and physical development, the development of a sound mind in a sound body, the training of reason to form just judgements, the disciplining of the will and affections to obey the supreme law of duty, the kindling and strengthening of the love of knowledge, of beauty, of goodness, till they become governing motives of action.

From Dorothea Beale *On the Education of Women* published in 1871

The curriculum at Cheltenham Ladies' College was sufficiently traditional to appease worried parents (dancing, music and painting, for example) and sufficiently radical to appease those parents looking for something radical for their daughters. The curriculum, always expanding, contained by the end of the century such subjects as scripture, languages, grammar, arithmetic, geography, botany, zoology and hockey.

Source P

[The school aimed to provide] an education based upon religious principles which, preserving the modesty and gentleness of the female character, should so far cultivate a girls' intellectual powers as to fit her for the discharge of those responsible duties which devolve upon her as a wife, mother, mistress and friend, the natural companion and helpmate for men.

The aims of the school, quoted in Elizabeth Raikes *Dorothea Beale of Cheltenham* published in 1908

Source Q

8.5 A photograph of a botany lesson at Cheltenham Ladies' College in 1895

SKILLS BUILDER

How far did the education supplied to girls at Cheltenham Ladies' College reflect the 'separate spheres' philosophy?

Cheltenham Ladies' College, unsurprisingly because it was a boarding school, deliberately catered for a more socially elite section of society than the North London Collegiate School. So, too, did the schools that followed its example: St Leonard's (in Scotland), Roedean and Wycombe Abbey.

What were the differences between Frances Mary Buss and Dorothea Beale?

The two women were pioneers in the field of education for women. They were friends and had a deep and lasting respect for each other's work. Yet they were very different.

Source R

(i) Miss Beale avoided problems of finance to a large extent by ensconcing herself in a highly privileged institution. She herself was from a secure background; she knew nothing of personal financial anxiety. Her tastes were frugal and she devoted large personal sums of money to the College and towards helping needy students. But Cheltenham was a highly select institution from the beginning – the credentials of prospective parents were carefully scrutinised and the Council determinedly rejected the 'daughters of trade'. The enormous increase in prestige which the College achieved during Miss Beale's headship rendered it even more privileged and secure. Miss Beale did not need to sully herself with the dubious business of financial appeals and her social propriety remained untarnished.

(ii) In marked contrast to Miss Beale, Miss Buss constantly muddied her boots, her hands and her reputation with sordid public appeals. She knew all about penny-pinching and the struggle to make ends meet: her background had not been as secure as Dorothea Beale's and her father's income had never sufficed to support his family. Frances Buss was a good entrepreneur. The North London Collegiate School which she founded was a highly successful commercial enterprise and until 1872, her own property. Miss Buss's restless ambitions and her zeal to do something about the education of girls not only of the relatively prosperous, but of the lower middle classes would never allow her to retreat into privilege as did Dorothea Beale. Miss Buss and a small group of friends begged and cajoled potential sympathisers for financial support, swallowing all their pride and suffering agonies of humiliation in the process. This was decidedly not ladylike behaviour and the antagonism, contempt and scorn that the public fund-raising brought was immense.

From Carole Dyhouse *Miss Buss and Miss Beale: Gender and Authority in the Field of Education* published in 1987

Question

Do you think Frances Mary Buss harmed the development of education for girls by her persistent fund-raising activities?

Definition

Trust

In the sense that the word is used here, it is a legal term referring to the way in which an organisation is set up and run. In this case, a group of people, called trustees, were set up to run a number of schools. This ensured that all schools in the Trust had the same aims and worked to the same principles.

What was the significance of the Girls' Public Day School Trust?

The establishment of the Girls' Public Day School Company (becoming a **Trust** in 1905) was one of the most important developments of the 1870s. Its object was to set up good and affordable day schools for girls and the scheme was first unveiled at a meeting in the Royal Albert Hall, London, in 1871. The prime movers behind the scheme were sisters Maria and Emily Shirreff and Mary Gurney; by 1873 the Trust was up and running. Their plan was to establish schools in response to local demand, and for local people to become shareholders in the company. In this way they had ownership of the schools in their towns. Official approval was not long in coming. Lady Stanley of Alderley and other peers, MPs and eminent men in the field of education were quick to give their support; HRH Princess Louise gave the royal seal of approval by agreeing to become the patron of the Company.

The North London Collegiate School was not a Trust school, (NLCS had been established for twenty-three years before the Trust got going) but was taken as the model for all Trust schools. GPDST schools spread rapidly throughout London and the provinces, to towns where there was no provision for the secondary education of girls. By 1898 the Trust had established thirty-four schools in places as far apart as Blackheath and Bath, Wimbledon and York, Norwich and Nottingham. The headmistresses of all GPDST schools were required to visit the North London Collegiate School before beginning their work, so that they could study teaching methods, the curriculum and the administration and organisation of the school.

Two other influential girls' schools were founded at this time:

- In 1874 Manchester High School was founded by a group of eminent Mancunians. They recorded that 'the rules and regulations for carrying on the North London Collegiate and Camden Schools were adopted as the basis of the permanent constitution of the High School.' In 1898, Sara Bustall, a former teacher at the North London Collegiate School, was appointed headmistress, and from this position exerted considerable influence on the development of girls' education in the north of England.

- In 1911 Dame Henrietta Barnett founded a school in her name in Hampstead, London. In doing so she leaned heavily on the advice of Sophie Bryant, who succeeded Frances Mary Buss as headmistress of the North London Collegiate School.

These new schools educated only a relatively small number of girls from middle-class families. In 1900, 70 per cent of middle-class girls who received any education outside their own homes received it in old-fashioned, privately owned small-scale academies. However, the 1902 Education Act resulted in over 1,000 new grammar schools being built by 1913 and the number of lower middle-class girls receiving an education did increase. By the time the First World War broke out, more and more local authorities were organising the education they provided along lines of ability rather than social class. Over half the places in state grammar schools were filled by children from the working class, and around half of these were girls.

What next? How easy was it for young women to go to university?

There was little point in educating girls so that they succeeded in public examinations if those who were able to could not carry their education forward and attend the country's universities. The provision of higher education for young women had always been considered as being the final blow to the 'angel in the house' and the ending of the 'separate spheres' philosophy. This was because it was believed that the possession of a university degree would open the professions to women and alter for ever the relationships between men and women within marriage. That was the theory. Reality was somewhat different. There was still a great deal of opposition to higher education for women, and still a great deal of prejudice for women to overcome.

Source S

The education of girls need not be of the same extended, classical, and commercial character as that of boys; they need more an education of the heart and feelings, and especially of firm, fixed, moral principles. They should be made conversant with history, geography, figures, the poets, and general literature, with a sure groundwork of religion and obedience. The profoundly educated women rarely make good wives or mothers. The pride of knowledge does not amalgamate well with the every-day matter of fact rearing of children, and women who have stored their minds with Latin and Greek seldom have much knowledge of pies and puddings, nor do they enjoy the hard and uninteresting work of attending to the wants of little children; but those women, poor things, who have lost their most attractive charm of womanliness, and are seen on the public platforms, usurping the exclusive duties of men, are seldom seen in their nurseries; though they may become notorious themselves, their children rarely do them credit, and the energy they throw away upon the equalising bubble, would be much better expended in a more womanly and motherly manner, in looking after their husbands' comforts, the training of their children, and the good of the household at large.

From Sarah Sewell *Women and the Times We Live In* published in 1868

Question

How might Frances Mary Buss or Dorothea Beale have answered Sarah Sewell?

The beginnings of higher education for young women

University education for young women began in the mid-nineteenth century:

1848   Queen's College London was founded to educate middle-class women to become governesses and teachers and governed by men.

1849   Bedford College London founded to offer women a full liberal arts education and included women on its governing body. Mainly used by women wishing to become teachers.

1878   University of London opened its degrees to women. Bedford, Westfield and Royal Holloway became constituent colleges (for women only) of the university.

The great municipal universities, Manchester and Leeds, for example, admitted women, too. But what women really wanted was that the two élite universities, Oxford and Cambridge, would open their doors to women as well.

What was the problem with Oxford and Cambridge?

The problem with Oxford and Cambridge was that they carried great symbolic weight because of their worldwide renown. In reality, however, the campaign to admit women was part of a larger campaign to turn Oxford and Cambridge into first-class research and teaching institutions rather than places where gentlemen pursued classical studies in a more or less relaxed manner.

The campaigns to make these two universities open to women were spearheaded by Elizabeth Garrett Anderson, Dorothea Beale, Barbara Bodichon, Frances Mary Buss and Emily Davies. These women, and others, founded the North of England Council for Promoting the Higher Education of Women, the London National Society for Women's Suffrage, the Society for Promoting the Employment of Women and *The Englishwoman's Journal*. Local organisations, too, supported women's entry into higher education. Many towns had ladies' Educational Associations and local businessmen pledge financial support. Through determination and steady, persistent pressure, concessions were gradually won.

In the late 1860s a house was purchased in Hitchin for women students and in 1872 this moved to Girton, a small village outside Cambridge. Girton College, as it became, was run by the redoubtable Emily Davis. In 1871 Henry Sidgewick and Millicent Garret Fawcett opened another college exclusively for women called Newnham, which was placed in the charge of Anne Jemima Clough. Most university professors gave Girton and Newnham students permission to attend lectures (with the important exception of the professors of Medicine), the students were allowed to take university examinations and received official certification for so doing – but not degrees. In 1879 Oxford University followed Cambridge's lead and opened two women's colleges: Lady Margaret Hall and Somerville.

Just look at this photograph in Source T. It doesn't look as though women were particularly welcome as students at Cambridge University!

Questions

- What would women students have felt, facing this demonstration?
- How would a male student explain why he got involved in this demonstration?

Source T

8.6 A photograph of a demonstration in 1897 against the admission of women to Cambridge University. Year after year attempts were made to admit women as full members of the university and year after year they failed. It was not until 1920 and 1947 respectively that Oxford and Cambridge admitted women to full membership.

Source U

Man is afraid of woman. He proves it every day. History proves it for him – the history of politics, the history of industry, the history of social life. An examination of women's present position and of men's attitude towards the women's movement shows evidence of fear at every turn. Man is afraid of woman because he has oppressed her. There is always for him the fear that the end may come, and rebellion carries with it not merely the throwing off of the yoke but alongside of it the dread of such vengeful retaliation as corresponds to the oppressor's tyranny.

From Teresa Billington Grieg *Women's Liberty and Men's Fear* published in 1907

SKILLS BUILDER

How valid do you find Teresa Billington-Grieg's explanation in Source U when it is applied to Source T?

Why was medicine such a difficult subject to study at university?

Medical faculties were generally much more conservative, and therefore more opposed to admitting women, than any of the others. Coupled to this was the general distaste felt about women attending classes in anatomy and physiology, particularly if they were taught in mixed classes.

Source V

I have a strong conviction that the entrance of ladies into dissecting rooms and anatomical theatres is undesirable in every respect, and highly unbecoming. It is not necessary that fair ladies should be brought into contact with such foul scenes – nor would it be for their good, any more than for that of their patients, if they could succeed in leaving the many spheres of usefulness which God has pointed out to them in order to force themselves into competition with the lower walks of the medical profession.

A hospital doctor explains to Elizabeth Garrett Anderson why he is opposed to women medical students. Quoted in Jo Manton *Elizabeth Garrett Anderson* published in 1965.

Yet force themselves they did. Elizabeth Blackwell was born in London but her family moved to America where she qualified as a doctor in 1849. Her name was placed on the British Medical Register in 1859. But the following year the medical profession secured a new charter enabling it to refuse registration to holders of foreign degrees. Elizabeth Garrett Anderson, sister of Millicent Fawcett, became the first woman, born and brought up in Britain, to be placed on the Medical Register and this happened in 1865; Sophia Jex-Blake followed her in 1877. Both women, forbidden entry to British medical schools, followed circuitous and very different routes to achieve their aim.

Elizabeth Garrett Anderson was able to register by first qualifying for an apothecary's licence (something not forbidden to women) and then using this to obtain entry to a medical degree course in Paris. The apothecary loophole was closed once she had used it (because it was this and not her foreign degree that got her onto the Register), and the four women who had passed the preliminary examination of the Apothecaries' Society were left high and dry.

Sophia Jex-Blake preferred a more frontal attack, aiming for a British medical degree. She and seven other women enrolled at Edinburgh University, where they encountered a great deal of hostility. In 1870, male medical students physically barred them from the anatomy rooms, the authorities denied them access to clinical training and so they could not complete their degrees. Forced to complete her medical education outside mainland Britain, in 1877 Sophia sat her examinations in Dublin, at the Irish College of Physicians.

Women medical students were greatly helped by the Enabling Act, passed in 1876, by which all medical institutions were ordered to admit women to their examinations, regardless of the terms of their Charters.

By the end of the nineteenth century, the idea was growing that well-educated women made better wives and mothers than poorly educated ones. It was also becoming accepted that women working in higher education did not have to be married and so the lack of a husband was no longer a symptom of failure. By 1900, only 15 per cent of university students in Britain were women; by 1939 this had risen to 23 per cent. For the few, the gates of all professions were beginning to creak open.

Unit summary

What have you learned in this unit?

You have learned that considerable strides were made during this period to ensure that girls were educated. Girls from poor working-class families gained from the legislation that made education in elementary schools compulsory and free, and from the earlier legislation providing for state-sponsored elementary schools when the provision of church-sponsored schools was inadequate. Although after 1902 it was possible for the daughters of poor families to gain scholarships to the new state secondary schools, this was a rare achievement. However, the ladder of opportunity had been created. The pioneer work of Dorothea Beale and Frances Mary Buss resulted in the daughters of middle-class parents having access to an education that was new, radical and which would equip them not only to be better wives and mothers, but to have the potential to embark on careers of their own. In order to do this, universities had to admit women, and this was happening gradually throughout the period. However, two systems of schooling had been set up: state sponsored for the poor, and private, fee paying for the well-to-do. This dual system was to last for many years. The spectre of the 'angel in the house' and the philosophy of 'separate spheres' continued to dog any moves by women and their male supporters to move towards equality of opportunity.

What skills have you used in this unit?

You have used a range of source material to explore the development of educational provision for girls and you have evaluated the differences in the provision for the daughters of the poor and the daughters of the middle class. This evaluation will have led you to understand that girls (and most particularly working-class girls) learned more than their lessons: they learned their place in society. You will have cross-referenced between sources dealing with the education of working-class girls and that being developed for middle-class girls and you will have understood how and why a dual system (fee-paying and state-funded) began. A study of sources relating to the willingness of universities to admit young women will have enabled you to use the skill of empathy to appreciate that the philosophy of 'separate spheres' was far from dead.

SKILLS BUILDER

1 How far did legislation concerning education in the years 1870–1902 enforce the 'separate spheres' philosophy?

2 Who contributed more to the education of girls at this time: Dorothea Beale or Frances Mary Buss?

3 Look at Source T.

   Given what you know about the personal and legal status of women by 1897, are you surprised at this reaction to the proposed entry of women to Cambridge University?

Exam tips

This is the sort of question you will find appearing on the examination paper as an (a) question.

4 Study Sources S, T and U.

How far does Source U support the views expressed in Source S and the actions portrayed in Source T?

You tackled (a) style questions at the end of Units 1 and 3. Now let's develop what you learned there about approaches to the (a) question.

- What is the question asking you to do? It is asking **how far** Source U **supports** Sources S and T.
- Consider the sources carefully and make **inferences** and **deductions** from them rather than using them as sources of information. You might put these inferences in three columns.
- **Cross-reference** points of evidence from the three sources by drawing actual links between evidence in the three columns. This will enable you to make comparisons point by point and so use the sources as a **set**.
- **Evaluate** the evidence, assessing its quality and reliability in terms of how much weight it will bear and how secure are the conclusions that can be drawn from it.
- Reach a **judgement** about how far Source U can be said to support Sources S and T.

Biography

Frances Mary Buss (1827–94)

Born in London, the eldest of ten children (five of whom survived to adulthood) of Robert Buss and Frances Fleetwood. Robert Buss was an unsuccessful engraver and the family were often close to poverty. Frances Mary attended a local free school and, when she was fourteen, was asked to stay on to teach the younger children. Inspired by her daughter's success, Mrs Buss opened her own school. Frances Mary:

- taught the older children at her mother's school;
- in 1849 attended Queen's College as an evening student in order to improve her teaching skills;
- in 1850 founded the North London Collegiate School for Ladies and remained its headmistress (the first person to use the name) until her death;
- employed only qualified teachers and occasionally visiting lecturers from Queen's College;
- turned North London Collegiate School into a flagship school for those involved in improving girls' education, including Emily Davies who later persuaded the authorities to allow women to become students at London university;
- worked with Emily Davies to gain permission for girls to be entered for the Oxford and Cambridge public examinations;
- in 1865 gave evidence to the Schools Enquiry Commission;
- in 1865 joined with Elizabeth Garrett Anderson, Dorothea Beale, Barbara Bodichon, Emily Davies and Helen Taylor to form a women's discussion group, the Kensington Society;
- was a member of the Kensington Society, which in 1866 formed the London Suffrage Committee and began organising a petition asking parliament for female enfranchisement;
- worked with Josephine Butler in her campaign against the Contagious Diseases Act;
- in 1871 turned North London Collegiate School from a private school into an endowed grammar school, able to offer scholarships to clever daughters from families who could not afford private school fees.

Biography

Dorothea Beale (1831–1906)

Born in London, the daughter of Miles Beale and Dorothea Complin, the fourth of twelve children. Her father was a surgeon and the family was comfortably off. After several unsuccessful attempts to find a governess for her, Dorothea was sent to school and then to Paris for a year. In 1848 she returned to England and enrolled as a day student at Queen's College, Harley Street, London, where she was appointed as their first Mathematics tutor. Dorothea then:

- in 1856 became head teacher of the Clergy Daughters' School in Casterton, Cumbria;
- in 1857 wrote *Textbook of General History*;
- in 1858 was appointed Head Teacher of Cheltenham Ladies College, which became a highly regarded (and expensive) academic boarding school for girls. Continued as head teacher until her death;
- played a prominent role in the Head Mistresses' Association and The Teachers' Guild;
- in 1865 joined with Elizabeth Garrett Anderson, Frances Mary Buss, Barbara Bodichon, Emily Davies and Helen Taylor to form a women's discussion group, the Kensington Society;
- became a member of the Kensington Society, which in 1866 formed the London Suffrage Committee and began organising a petition asking parliament for female enfranchisement;
- became vice-president of the Central Society for Women's Suffrage;
- in 1892 founded St Hilda's College, Oxford, for women only;
- presided over St Hilda's in 1897, being accepted by the Association for Promoting the Higher Education of Women as being of a high standard;
- wrote several books about education, including *Work and Play in Girls' Schools*.

RESEARCH TASK

Dorothea Beale's first school as head teacher was Casterton School in Cumbria. This school figures as Lowood School in Charlotte Brontë's *Jane Eyre*.

- Find a copy of Jane Eyre, by Charlotte Brontë.

- Note down all the references to Lowood Hall.

- How far do you think Lowood Hall accurately represents schools at this time? Use the sources from this unit and your own knowledge in your answer.

9 Opening up the world of work

What is this unit about?

This unit focuses on the changing work opportunities for girls and women during this period. It considers the reasons why these opportunities changed and how they developed. The differences in the work opportunities for working-class and middle-class girls and women are addressed. The impact of the First World War is considered, as are the changing attitudes of the trade unions, the public and women themselves to the opening of workplace opportunities for girls and women.

Key questions

- How far had the job opportunities for girls and women changed throughout the period?
- To what extent had the 'separate spheres' philosophy been overturned by the changing role of women in the workplace?

Timeline

1857	sewing machine invented: increase in volume of work done in the 'sweated trades' at home
1867	Agricultural Gangs Act bans employment of young girls
1874	Factory Act introduces a maximum ten-hour working day for women in factories outside the textile industry first typewriters sold in Britain
1875	women make up more than 50 per cent of all elementary school teachers Emma Paterson founds the Women's Protective and Provident League
1878	Factory and Workshop Act extends protection for women and young people to all industries
1879	introduction of the telephone extends range of clerical work done by women and opens up new jobs in the Post Office, for example
1888	Annie Besant organises the first women's strike at Bryant and May's match factory
1893	women allowed to become factory inspectors
1896	Factory Act bans the employment of children under eleven. Women are not to be employed for four weeks after having a child
1901	Factory Act reduces by one hour the time a woman can work each day
1906–13	series of Shops Acts establishes sixty-four-hour working week for shop work

1909	Trade Boards Act settles rate of earnings in four trades: box-making, lace-making, chain-making and tailoring
1914–18	women and girls take on a wide range of occupations previously regarded as being exclusively male
1915	Women's War Register set up
Right to Work march
1919	Sex Disqualification (Removal) Act made it illegal to bar women from jobs just because of their gender
Restoration of Pre-War Practices Act guarantees a return to pre-war working practices for both men and women.

Source A

9.1 A picture called *Dinner Hour, Wigan* painted by Eyre Crowe in 1874

Questions

- What immediate impression do you get from this painting about the lives of the young women operatives?
- How old do you think they are? How would they have been affected by legislation regarding their personal lives?
- What sort of education would these young women have probably experienced?
- Does anything about this picture surprise you?

Look carefully at the painting. The artist visited northern towns and painted what he saw. These young women are enjoying a dinner-hour break from their work in the cotton mills of Wigan.

How far did women's jobs change in the years before the first world war?

A major problem in looking at changes and continuity in women's work is that there is very little firm evidence on which to base any conclusions. A lot of the evidence is anecdotal; statistics, where they can be gathered, are unreliable, and some women's work, for a variety of reasons, tended to go unnoticed and so unrecorded. However, when all the evidence is taken together as a package, certain trends can be detected.

Source B

	Women aged 15+ at work (to the nearest 1000)	Women workers as per cent of the total female population
1851	2,348,200	25.7
1861	2,709,900	26.3
1871	3,118,200	26.8
1881	3,393,600	25.4

From Charles Booth *Journal of the Royal Historical Society* published in 1886 showing women and girls at work 1851–81

The figures in Source B were taken from the censuses, which took place (and still do) every ten years. They show a remarkable, and perhaps surprising, consistency. Indeed, when the figures are re-worked to show women workers as a percentage of the entire workforce, in 1851 women workers constituted 30.2 per cent and in 1901, 29.1 per cent of all those in work.

Census data has been used to compile these statistics, and here care has to be taken. The enumerators simply wrote down what they were told when they visited each household on a specific day in March or April. Many women undertook casual domestic work, taking in washing and mending, for example, or sold food from their front rooms, or undertook seasonal agricultural work or helped in the family business. None of this would be counted as 'work' by the **enumerator** and, probably, not even mentioned by the person giving the enumerator the information he needed. The work of many women, and particularly working-class married women, went unrecorded.

However, when the given occupations of the workers are analysed, an interesting picture emerges.

Definition

Enumerator

Literally, an enumerator is a person who counts. In this context, an enumerator was the person who took the census. Enumerators visited every house on census night and listed everyone who was living there with, after 1851, details of where they were born and what work they did.

Source C

Occupation	1851	1881	1911
Agriculture, horticulture	229	116	117
Textiles	635	745	870
Metal manufacture, machines	36	49	128
Clothing	491	667	825
Food, drink, tobacco	53	98	308
Domestic services	1135	1756	2127
Professional occupations	103	203	383
Commercial operations	0	11	157
Public administration	3	9	50
Paper, printing	16	53	144

The main occupations of women of all ages in Great Britain in 1851, 1881 and 1911 in thousands. Taken from A. John (ed.) *Unequal Opportunities: Women's Employment in England 1800–1918* published in 1985.

1 Which occupation showed the biggest percentage increase, 1851–1911?

2 Can you suggest why this should have been?

Domestic service: a case study

Domestic service occupied the largest number of girls and women throughout the period. The work was hard and unregulated, long and poorly paid. Nevertheless, it was regarded as suitable work for working-class girls and an excellent preparation for their role in life as wives and mothers.

Source D

Female domestic servants discharge a most important and indispensable function in social life; they do not follow an obligatory independent, and therefore for their sex an unnatural, career. On the contrary, they are attached to others and are connected to other existences, which they embellish, facilitate, and serve. In a word, they fulfil both essentials of woman's being: they are supported by, and they minister to, men. We could not possibly do without them.

From the *National Review* published in April 1862

SKILLS BUILDER

How far does this view about domestic service reflect the 'angel in the house' and the 'separate spheres' philosophies?

Domestic work may have given working-class girls the security of a roof over their heads and regular meals on the table, but there were huge drawbacks. If a servant lost her place, she lost her home as well. Most servants were required to live in and to remain unmarried and childless. Many were seen by the males of the household as being sexually available; pregnant domestic servants were inevitably dismissed and had to hide the fact of their childbearing if they were to get another place. Their free time was limited; boyfriends were frowned upon and the loss of any sort of social life was what most women in domestic service regretted. On the other hand, annual contracts freed domestic servants from the worry of seasonal unemployment. And because of the status symbol conferred on the growing middle classes by the possession of a servant, work of this kind was never hard to find.

Source E

The situation of a domestic servant is attended with considerable comfort. With abundant work, it combines a wonderful degree of liberty, discipline, health, physical comfort, good example, regularity, room for advancement, encouragement to acquire saving habits. The most numerous class of depositors in the Savings Bank is that of domestic servants. The situation frequently involves much responsibility, and calls forth the best features of character. Kind attachment in return for honest service is not uncommon with the master or mistress; and an honest pride in the relationship springs up on both sides and lasts throughout life.

From J.D. Milne *The Industrial and Social Position of Women* published in 1857

However, not everyone would agree.

Source F

No amount of kindness, or even of genial companionship, on the part of master and mistress, can compensate the female servants from being cut off from an independent social life. And what is offered to them instead? They are connected with the wealthier classes principally as ministering to their material well-being. They have a clear and complete view of their luxury. No people contemplate so frequently and so strikingly the unequal distribution of wealth: they fold up dresses whose price contains double the amount of their years' wages; they pour out at dinner wine whose cost would have kept a poor family for weeks. And of the amusements and occupations, of the higher interests and of the higher life of the leisured classes, of which comfort and ease and luxury is only supposed to be the basis, they have no share and, probably, no understanding. Cut off from their own general life, they remain spectators from the outside of that of others. What they gain by constant association with the wealthier classes are, principally, external qualities – politeness, a certain amount of outward refinement, a high standard of cleanliness for themselves and of comfort for others. Sometimes they find patron, but rarely a friend.

From *The Nineteenth Century*, a popular quarterly magazine, published in August 1890

Source G

In all but large, rich households where there is much idleness and waste, domestic service is incessant hard work at all hours of the day and sometimes of the night also. It is at the best but a kind of slavery and when a girl has a home, it is only a human feeling (and one we should respect) if she prefers to undertake work in trades because she can return at night and on Sundays to the home circle. At a meeting last year of factory women in Bristol who were earning only five shillings or six shillings a week, I urged upon them the advisability of going out to service rather than submit to such low wages. But without an exception, the advice was rejected by all.

From Emma Paterson *The Woman's Union Journal* published in 1879. Emma was a middle-class feminist and founder of the Women's Protective and Provident League, which aimed to support working women.

Even so, by 1881, one in every three girls aged between fifteen and twenty were employed as domestics in households other than their own. This figure, however, varied from town to town and region to region as well as across time. In York, for example, in 1851, 60 per cent of employed women were in domestic service; in Preston, which had a flourishing textile industry, the figure was nearer 3 per cent. It would seem that where there was a choice, young women preferred factory work. Why?

What was the lure of factory work?

By 1899, over half a million women worked in factories. These were concentrated, of course, in the great industrialised towns and cities of northern England, the Midlands and South Wales, where the female population provided a crucial source of workers. These women may have been paid less than if they had been in domestic service (and certainly were when the domestic servant's board and lodging were taken into account) but to be paid a wage and to work away from the home environment gave them an independence they could not otherwise have achieved.

Look again at Source A. The workforce in the Lancashire cotton mills were comprised mainly of young, single women like these. Indeed, the prosperity of the cotton industry was dependent upon these women operatives. But it wasn't only in the textile industries that women made their mark. The invention of the bicycle, for example, and its growing acceptance of cycling as a suitable activity for women, provided job opportunities too.

Question

The women are clearly working. But what are the men doing?

Source H

9.2 A photograph of women workers in a cycle factory in Coventry in the 1890s. The 'safety' bicycle was invented in 1885, so this is a modern development.

How important were technological inventions in changing women's working lives?

The introduction of the telephone and the typewriter into the workplace had a profound effect on job opportunities.

Remington typewriters were sold in England from 1874 but it wasn't until the 1880s that their introduction impacted on the business world. Typewriting was likened to piano-playing and quickly came to be seen as the exclusive province of women. Women with typing skills, especially when coupled with shorthand, were very much in demand in the expanding world of business and commerce.

The telephone and the telegraph provided thousands of job opportunities for women. By 1914 the Post Office was the largest single employer of middle-class women in the country and accounted for 90 per cent of all the women employed by the central government.

The 1881 census recorded 6,000 women working as clerks in private companies. By 1901 this had risen to 60,000, and by 1914, clerical workers were ranked third in the list of popular occupations for middle-class women, behind shop workers and teachers.

Why was shop work so popular?

The end of the nineteenth century saw a revolution in the production of retail goods. Standardised, mass-produced branded articles became the norm. These could be sold by anyone, and the days of the specialised, small-scale trader with no need for shop assistants, were numbered. This was coupled with the development of department stores. William Whitely, advertising his store as the 'universal provider' opened a great department store in London in 1863; David Lewis, opening a store in Liverpool, described himself and his staff as 'friends of the people'. By the 1900s, chains of shops had developed. Jesse Boot, the Northamptonshire chemist, owned some 181 shops; Thomas Lipton, the grocer, had more than sixty shops in London alone and others throughout the country.

These developments provided acceptable work for lower middle-class women. It has been estimated that in 1875 there were 295,000 shops in Britain, and that by 1907 this number had risen to 459,952. The work was clean, respectable, and certainly not manual; shop owners demanded that the women they employed dressed modestly and spoke well. Clearly there were plenty of openings here for women wanting 'respectable' work. The hours, however, were long with small shops in suburbs tending to stay open for longer than large ones in city centres. For some women shop workers, an 85-hour week was not uncommon. Nevertheless, to be a shop assistant was clearly more popular than service and factory work, which were increasingly seen as the province of the working classes.

Did women enter the professions?

The three professions most prized by women were teaching, medicine and the law. All three required higher education, and you have read in Unit 8 about the problems women faced in gaining access to college and university.

Secondary school teaching was the occupation of choice for most girls from middle-class families anxious to follow a career. It was deemed eminently suitable by society: it enabled the women to use their education while at the same time not compromising on their perceived femininity. Furthermore, it did not put women in competition with men. Grammar school teachers trained at women's colleges and worked in schools for girls; some worked in boarding schools or returned to teach in all-female colleges – all of which was seen as a natural complement to women's domestic role. Sara Burstall, for example, attended the North London Collegiate School as a girl, returning there to teach after attending Girton College Cambridge and crowning her career by becoming head mistress of Manchester High School for Girls.

The legal profession remained closed to women until after the First World War. Women wanting to become barristers and solicitors had to wait until the Sex Disqualification (Removal) Act (1919), which made it illegal to bar women from jobs just because of their gender.

Medicine remained problematic for some time. The nursing profession had organised and re-organised itself since Florence Nightingale's work in the Crimean War (1854–6) and towards the end of the nineteenth century it was considered a respectable profession for girls to enter. The problem, of course, was that nursing required a certain intimacy with the bodies of strangers – including men – and various messy procedures and processes. When more hospitals were built in the 1880s, and therefore more nurses were required, hospital administrators 'solved' the problem by appointing upper middle-class women as managing sisters and lower middle-class women as working nurses. Thus class differentials were maintained and niceties observed.

For doctors it was somewhat different. Unit 8 has described the main obstacles put in the way of women wishing to become doctors, and throughout the period medicine was the highest-status profession women aspired to enter. It was here that they challenged male perceptions about their role and abilities. In 1874, Elizabeth Garrett Anderson and Sophia Jex-Blake (see page 143) opened the London School of Medicine for Women, determined to show that women could meet the medical needs of other women. In doing so they were attempting to carve out a separate niche for women instead of arguing that they were capable of doing male doctor's work on equal terms with men. The satirical magazine *Punch* pointed out the ludicrous nature of the situation.

Source I

THE COMING RACE.

Doctor Evangeline. "By the bye, Mr. Sawyer, are you engaged to-morrow afternoon? I have rather a ticklish Operation to perform—an Amputation, you know."

Mr. Sawyer. "I shall be very happy to do it for you."

Dr. Evangeline. "O, no, not THAT! But will you kindly come and administer the Chloroform for me?'

9.3 From the magazine *Punch* published on 14 August 1872

SKILLS BUILDER

Is *Punch* in favour of women doctors, or not?

Even so, by 1900 there were only two hundred women on the Medical Register, and by 1914, one thousand, not all of whom were able to find work after qualifying.

How far did government legislation help working women?

The nineteenth and early twentieth centuries saw a plethora of Acts of Parliament aimed at regulating people's working conditions. The earliest legislation applied only to the cotton industry, but gradually, beginning with the Mines Act of 1842, legislation extended to other industries and workplaces. No legislation was specifically aimed at women, although clauses in larger Acts did relate to them. Indeed, women tended to be put together with children as being two groups of vulnerable people needing protection, rather than with men and considered as adults requiring equality of treatment.

- 1867 Agricultural Gangs Act

  It was common in East Anglia for a 'gang-master' to guarantee to a landowner that a specific job would be completed in a certain number of days and for an agreed fee. The gang-master would then assemble a gang of workers, pay them to do the work and pocket the profit. This Act required every gang-master to be licensed by the local council for periods of six months at a time, and to be of good character. It forbade women to be employed in the same gangs as men and forbade them to work under a male gang-master. Women could only work in all-women gangs under a woman gang-master.

- 1867 Workshops' Regulations Act

  Workplaces with fewer than fifty people were forbidden to employ girls and boys under eight years old, and children aged between eight and thirteen could only work part-time. Young people and women were restricted to a twelve-hour day with one and a half hours allowed for meal breaks. Children, young people and women were not to be employed after 2p.m. on Saturdays in establishments with more than five employees, and child employees were to attend school for ten hours a week.

- 1874 Factory Act

  This Act raised the minimum working age for boys and girls to nine years; limited the working day to ten hours for women and young people in the textile industry, these hours to be between 6a.m. and 6p.m.; and reduced the working week to $56\frac{1}{2}$ hours.

- 1886 Shop Hours Regulation Act

  Regulated the hours of girls and boys and young persons to a maximum of 74 per week, including meal times. This was repeated and strengthened in 1892 by requiring local councils to inspect shops.

- 1896 Factory Act

  This Act banned the employment in factories of girls and boys under the age of 11. Employers were not permitted knowingly to employ a woman within four weeks of her giving birth.

- 1901 Factory Act

  This was a major consolidation of previous Acts. The minimum working age for girls and boys was raised to twelve; the number of hours a woman could work was reduced by one.

- 1906–14 Shop Hours Regulation Acts

  A number of minor Acts succeeded in establishing a maximum of sixty-four hours a week for shop work

It was, of course, one thing to pass legislation and quite another to enforce it. It would, too, be wrong to assume that all women were pleased with the legislation and the ways in which it affected them.

SKILLS BUILDER

For each of these Acts, work out why women might (a) have welcomed them and (b) criticised them.

Source J

The hours of employment permissible under the 1901 Factory Act were long. Women and girls over fourteen years old could be employed 12 hours a day and on Saturday 8 hours. In addition, in certain industries, and dressmaking was one, an additional 2 hours could be worked by women on 30 nights in any 12 months.

Workrooms were often overcrowded, dirty, ill-ventilated, and insufficiently heated. The employment of little errand girls, usually only fourteen years of age, soon attracted my attention. Their work was very varied – running errands, matching materials, taking out parcels, cleaning the workrooms, and often also helping in the work of the house. To be at the beck and call of all employed in a busy workshop was arduous and fatiguing. They could work legally from 8am to 8pm, and often were sent out from the workshop a few minutes before 8pm to take a dress to a customer living some distance away, which resulted in their not reaching home until a late hour. It was not surprising that the young persons in those workshops often looked weary and overdone; but there were plenty of girls to take their place, so they would not give in.

In 1901 Helen Martindale became a factory inspector. She later wrote about her experiences in *From One Generation to Another*. Here she describes her visits to dressmakers' workrooms. If you look back to the Introduction, you will see that Agnes Crane worked for a dressmaker before she married.

Questions

- Why do you think the main focus of the Factory Acts was on hours of work, not working conditions?
- What could be done to improve working conditions?

How far did trade unions help working women?

Male workers in a wide range of trades and industries had been organising and re-organising themselves into trade societies and trade unions, with varying degrees of success, throughout the nineteenth century. Their aims were to protect their pay, their jobs and to try to obtain better working conditions for themselves. When women became, through sheer force of numbers, serious contributors to working life, they also became, in many ways, men's competitors.

Women's wages as a challenge to men?

Source K

Industry	Female earnings as per cent of male earnings
Textiles	58.5
Clothing	46.3
Food, drink, tobacco	41.5
Paper, printing	36.4
Metal industries	38.1
Total (of all industries)	43.7

The average earnings of women as a percentage of male earnings, 1906

Although job opportunities for women had increased dramatically, they were paid considerably less than men. Not only was this a problem for the women themselves, it was also a problem for male trade unionists. Would the women, with their lower pay, undercut them and take their jobs? Would the low pay of women force down the pay of their male colleagues? Were there other reasons why male trade unions were not happy supporting women in the workplace?

Problems with trade unionism

Source L

It was their duty as men and husbands to use their utmost efforts to bring about a condition of things where their wives should be in their proper sphere at home, seeing after their house and family, instead of being dragged into the competition for livelihood against the great and the strong men of the world.

Part of an address to the Trades Union Congress, made by its President, Henry Broadhurst, in 1877

Source M

Mr Sedgewick (Birmingham) said that wherever female labour in his trade had been introduced, the wages of men had been reduced by one half. He refused to bind himself to support a movement that would make such a result more general.

Mr H.D. Richardson stated that what the men objected to was to allow women to manufacture the same articles as the men at half the cost. They were perfectly willing to allow women to enter any trade, and produce any article as long as they did not work for a lower wage than the men.

Part of a TUC debate, reported in the *Women's Union Journal* published in 1877

Source N

The largest proportion of women wage earners do not organise because they look upon it as a temporary occupation to be superseded by marriage! They fail to see any need for bothering themselves about the wages and general conditions obtaining in their trade. Until girls are taught independence and a trade, women wage-earners in the aggregate will remain where they are today – outside the ranks of Trade Unionism.

From Margaret Bondfield, Assistant Secretary of the National Amalgamated Union of Shop Assistants writing in 1900

SKILLS BUILDER

1 Why did women have a problem with trade unionism?

2 Which of the reasons given in the above three sources do you think is the most important?

By the end of the nineteenth century, there were three ways in which women could become unionised. Some unions admitted women on the same terms as men. The union to which Margaret Bondfield belonged was one of these; some unions had separate women's sections within a union that was essentially run by men, and other unions were run by women for women. Many male trade unionists gave generously of their time and expertise to help women set up their own unions. A Mr D. Merrick, for example, had helped set up the Leicester Union of Women Seamers and Stitchers and a Mr H.R. King had similarly helped to set up a London-based women's union in his trade, which was book-binding. By 1906, some 167,000 women were trade unionists, and this number had doubled by 1914.

The Women's Trade Union League

In 1875 Emma Paterson formed the Women's Protective and Provident League, the first union for women workers. It represented dressmakers, upholsterers, bookbinders, artificial flower makers, feather dressers, tobacco, jam and pickle workers, shop assistants and typists. In 1903 it changed its name to the Women's Trade Union League. The main objective of the League was to educate women about the advantages of trade union membership. It supported women's demands for better working conditions and helped to raise awareness about the exploitation of women workers.

Source O

How would you like to iron a shirt a minute? Think of standing at a mangle just above the washroom with the hot steam pouring up through the floor for 10, 12, 14 and sometimes 17 hours a day! Sometimes the floors are made of cement and then it seems as though one were standing on hot coals, and the workers are dripping with perspiration. They are breathing air laden with particles of soda, ammonia and other chemicals! The Laundry Workers Union in one city reduced this long day to 9 hours, and has increased the wages 50 per cent.

From a Women's Trade Union League pamphlet published in 1909

Did women trade unionists do any good?

Women trade unionists, no matter in which kind of organisation they were operating, had the well-being of women workers as their focus. They conducted surveys, reported, pressurised and did make a difference.

Definition

Sweated industries

Instead of giving a job to a craftsman, it would be handed over to a middleman or woman, known as a 'sweater'. He or she would take it round to the home of an unskilled worker, usually a woman, who would do the work for very low pay. Often this work was broken down into a series of small jobs, each attracting a very small amount of money.

Source P

The impact of low wages was made worse by the unreliability of work. A survey organised in the Manchester area in the mid 1890s of conditions in all-women industries, such as shirt-making and umbrella covering, showed that out of the hundred and twenty workers questioned, only three could always rely on a regular wage. The vast majority were on piecework, and, depending on how fast they worked, could earn anything between 3 shillings and 20 shillings; in slack periods few earned more than five shillings. At these starvation rates, commented the organisers of the survey, a woman had 'to use the largest stitch that will stand the inspection of the giver out of work'.

From a speech made by Frances Ashwell on a survey 'Conditions of Women's Wages in Manchester' given to the Women's Trade Union Council in July 1897. It was reported in the *Monthly Herald*, the local Co-operative paper, which was particularly interested because the Women's Co-operative Guild had taken part in the survey.

In 1906, as the climax of a number of similar investigations, the *Daily News* organised an exhibition of work in the **sweated industries**. Public outrage was sufficient for Trade Boards to be introduced in 1909, with the power to fix minimum wage rates in trades such as tailoring, box-making and chain-making.

Other women trade unionists went for direct action.

Source Q

Bryant and May, now a limited liability company, paid last year a dividend of 23 per cent to its shareholders.

The hour for commencing work is 6.30 in summer and 8 in winter; work concludes at 6pm. Half-an-hour is allowed for breakfast and an hour for dinner. This long day of work is performed by young girls, who have to stand the whole of the time. A typical case is that of a girl of 16, a piece worker who earns 4 shillings a week. Out of the earnings, 2 shillings is paid for the rent of a room. The child lives on only bread and butter and tea. The splendid salary of 4 shillings is subject to deductions in the shape of fines. If the feet are dirty, or the ground under the bench is left untidy, a fine of 3d is inflicted; for putting 'burnts' – matches that have caught fire during work – on the bench, 1 shilling had been forfeited. If a girl leaves four or five matches on her bench when she goes for a fresh 'frame' she is fined 3d, and in some departments a fine of 3d is imposed for talking. The wage covers the duty of submitting to an occasional blow from a foreman. These female 'hands' eat their food in the rooms in which they work, so that the fumes of the phosphorous mix with their poor meal and they eat disease as seasoning to their bread. Disease, I say: for the 'phossy jaw' that they talk about means caries of the jaw, and the phosphorous poison works on them as they chew their food, and rots away the bone.

From a newspaper article 'White Slavery' by Annie Besant, published in 1888. Here she is writing about girls who work in Bryant and May's match factory.

Annie Besant encouraged the girls to come out on strike and supported them throughout their action. Her articles in papers gained them widespread support and her connections with other unions, such as the Women's Trade Union League, brought money to help. Within three weeks, the match girls had won: the fines were stopped, their wages were increased and their working conditions were improved.

Biography

Clementina Black (1854–1922)

Born in Brighton in 1854, Clementina's father was David Black, a solicitor, and her mother was Maria Patten, a successful portrait painter. When Clementina was a child her father became seriously ill, losing the use of his legs, and her mother died in 1874. Clementina was left in charge of an invalid father and seven brothers and sisters. In whatever spare time she had, Clementina began writing. Her first novel *A Sussex Idyll* was published. After the death of her father, she moved to London where she continued writing. She:

- met Eleanor Marx, the daughter of Karl Marx, in 1886 and as a result joined the Women's Trade Union League and became its honorary secretary
- travelled Britain persuading women to join trade unions
- attended the Trades Union Congress in 1888 and moved a motion on equal pay for equal work
- was involved in the formation of the Consumers' League, an organisation that aimed to pressurise employers who paid low wages to women, and as a result supported Annie Besant and the match-girls' strike
- helped form the Women's Trade Union Association in 1889, which in 1894 joined forces with the Women's Industrial Council. She became president of the Council and for the next twenty years was involved in collecting and publicising information on womens' work.
- was a member of the Anti-Sweating League and organised conferences on the subject
- was an active member of the left wing Fabian Society and a member of the NUWSS; in 1912 she edited their journal *The Common Cause*
- continued to write novels until her death.

Biography

Emma Smith (Paterson after marriage) (1848–86)

Born in London in 1848, Emma's father was a headmaster who educated her at home. Apprenticed to a book-binder, on her father's death she turned to teaching, helping her mother run the school. Emma:

- became secretary to the Women's Suffrage Association in 1872
- married Thomas Paterson in 1873 and, during their honeymoon in America, became impressed by the women-only unions that were being established there
- once back in the UK, founded the Women's Protective and Provident League (later the Women's Trade Union League) with the aim of establishing unions in every trade in which women worked
- became, in 1875, with Edith Simcox the first women delegates to attend a Trades Union Congress and continued to attend regularly until her death
- was opposed to protective legislation exclusively for women, which she saw as restricting their access to higher paid jobs, and inappropriate when women had no political influence to frame such legislation
- co-founded and edited the *Women's Union Journal*.

To what extent did the First World War impact on job opportunities for women?

Women's work during the First World War was of inestimable value to the war effort and played a huge part in actually winning the war. Women were seen by the public as possessing the abilities needed to perform a large range of skilled and unskilled jobs, jobs that were physically demanding and jobs that required a high level of intelligence. But in reality, how far were women accepted in the workplace? And, perhaps more importantly, did any gains made during the war survive during the peacetime years that followed?

Unemployment and the 'Right to Work'

The outbreak of war proved disastrous for female employment. In 1914, before the outbreak of war, approximately 5 million women were at work. Before the end of September, some 190,000 had lost their jobs. Uncertain of what to expect and fearing a trade slump, Lancashire cotton mills laid off thousands of women; domestic service, the largest employer of women, was hit hard, too, as middle-class families, fearing a recession, tightened their belts. Working-class women and their families inevitably suffered. In order to help relieve the suffering, the Central Committee for Women's Employment set up the Queen's Work for Women Fund, under the patronage of Queen Mary. This offered a limited amount of re-training for London-based women by setting up workshops in Bethnal Green and Stepney where they were taught new trades. Much of the output from these workshops was for the army – socks, greatcoats, shirts and webbing belts, for example. The importance of this was that:

- the value of women's incomes to working-class families had been officially recognised; and

- the need to recompense women for withdrawal of these incomes had been recognised – if only in a very small way.

It was not until 1915, however, that the government seemed fully to realise the need to recruit women into the workforce. The enlistment of skilled workers had left vital industries, such as munitions, woefully and even dangerously short of labour. Both government and employers looked to the recruitment of women as an immediate, short-term solution to the problem.

It didn't take long for the government to realise that this potentially huge workforce needed organising and, perhaps more importantly, they needed to know what it could do. In the summer of 1915 they set up a Woman's War Register, and within two weeks, over 33,000 women had enrolled. The willingness of women to work was clear, and was emphasised by the 'Right to Work' march (see page 109).

Source R

THESE WOMEN ARE
DOING THEIR BIT

LEARN TO
MAKE
MUNITIONS

9.4 This recruitment poster
was issued by the Ministry
of Munitions in 1916

Source S

The two crucial phenomena which transformed the opportunities open to women,
at least for as long as the war lasted, were, first, the shortage of munitions which
led in May 1915 to the setting up of a special Ministry of Munitions, and, second,
the shortage of soldiers, which led in January 1916 to the conscription of single
men, and in May 1916 to universal male conscription. What becomes clear, too, is
that, far more than extreme feminists would allow, the changes affecting women
were very dependent upon changes affecting men.

From Arthur Marwick *Women at War 1914–1918* published in 1977

What work did women do?

Predominantly, women worked making munitions. One of the largest munitions factories was the Woolwich Arsenal in London. In 1914 it employed 125 women; by 1917, 25,000 women worked there. Women went into chemical and engineering industries, into banking, the civil service and clerical work. They took over the businesses of their male relatives, plumbing and decorating, window cleaning and coal delivering. They delivered the mail and worked as conductors on trams, ploughed fields and felled trees. As the war progressed, and particularly once skilled men were called up, it became clear that women had to be trained for more specialised jobs. For example, women trained as welders and fitters, as optical lens grinders for telescopes and periscopes, as gas fitters and plumbers and as gauge-makers for bomb fuses.

The trade unions and 'dilution'

Women training for skilled jobs worried the trade unions. They felt they needed to protect this skilled work for returning soldiers when the war was over. Consequently the government had to seek agreements and compromises with employers and trade unions. It was decided to split complex, skilled tasks into several sections. Whereas one man might have, pre-1914, completed a whole task (say, the turning and finishing of a shell), after 1914, two women would perform the same task. This 'dilution' of labour was, of course, a compromise for women. But it did enable them to begin to make an assault on the closed shop of skilled labour in industries hitherto closed to women. But not everyone was happy. While government, desperate to maintain a high level of industrial production, urged the employment of women, trade unions remained suspicious: the Amalgamated Society of Engineers, for example, continued to refuse to admit women because of the perceived threat to their livelihoods. Employers, too, regularly filed complaints to the Ministry of Reconstruction's Committee on Women in Industry, pointing out that married women regularly needed time off work due to childcare problems and domestic issues – and so were far from ideal employees.

The trade unions and equal pay

The problem of equal pay for equal work was one that dogged women's employment throughout the war and dominated negotiations afterwards. Women's wages in the same industry were a fraction of those earned by men (look back at Source K). Dilution enabled this discrimination to continue. Women were allocated to only part of a skilled job and so were paid less. The real problems came where men and women performed identical skilled work. Although government directives urged equal pay for equal work, this was difficult to achieve in practice, and women lacked the experience of industrial bargaining to force the issue. And the employers knew it.

Source T

9.5 Dilution in action: a young woman helps an older man operate a magazine drilling plate at the Tyneside shipbuilders Swan Hunter and Wigham Richardson

Something lost and something gained?

The war had forced both the government and the public at large to recognise the vital importance of the role played by women's work in bringing about victory. It forced the trade unions and employers to face up to the 'problem' of skilled women in the work place. In doing this, the whole underlying issue of whether or not a woman's place was in the home was brought to the fore. Maybe this was the only gain for women of their wartime experiences.

Source U

It is questionable whether women gained any significant long-term advantages from their wartime experiences. Certainly all the agreements with employers and trade unions had emphasised the importance of reinstating men to their jobs once the war had ended. Despite the expectation of suffragists that war must have changed men's opinions of women and that women would be able to maintain permanent jobs in skilled occupations, the demobilisation of women from wartime work was substantial. As Minister of Munitions, Lloyd George's definition of women's future role in society was unambiguous 'The workers of today are the mothers of tomorrow'. For many women wartime economic independence was short-lived as post-war government policies encouraged women to return to their domestic responsibilities.

From Annette Mayer *Women in Britain 1900–2000* published in 2002

To what extent were women affected by the return to a peacetime economy?

The demobilisation of three and a half million men had a dramatic affect on women's war-time employment. There was the very clear expectation among government, trade unions and the men themselves that a return to normal meant that women would revert to their domestic roles. It was a view shared by many, but by no means all, women.

How serious was female unemployment?

During the war, some four and a half million women had, quite literally, rolled up their sleeves and proved that they could be an effective workforce. Without women workers, the war would have been lost. Now that the men were back, and the British economy faced problems as it wound down from wartime levels of production, women workers were dispensable. Some 113,000 women were dismissed from their jobs within two weeks of the war ending; five months later, the total was 600,000. By 1921, the female industrial workforce had been reduced to 2 per cent lower than it had been in 1914.

What was the role of the unions and the government?

This reduction in the female workforce had been foreshadowed during the war. In the Treasury Agreement of 1915 with the trade unions, the government had agreed that 'dilution' would end once the war was over. So it was no surprise that the male-dominated trade union conference passed resolutions in 1918 demanding the reduction in hours of women's working days from twelve to eight on weekdays with just four hours on Saturdays. The 'separate spheres' philosophy that had so dominated the nineteenth century was clearly alive and well in the twentieth: the underlying assumption here was that industrial work was incompatible with family life. This view was reinforced in June 1919, when parliament passed the Pre-War Trade Practices Act, guaranteeing pre-war pay and conditions for women.

To what extent was the blow cushioned by the government?

Some attempt was made by the government to help unemployed women whose own domestic economy had been geared up to their wartime earnings:

- The out-of-work donation scheme gave women 25 shillings a week for thirteen weeks on condition that they reported to a labour exchange every day and were immediately available for work.

- In November 1919 this was reduced to 15 shillings a week.

- In 1920, the whole scheme was replaced by the Unemployed Insurance Act, which gave women 12 shillings a week, a rate lower than that for men. If a woman refused an offer of work, the benefit was withdrawn, even if that work was the widely disliked domestic service paying 6 shillings a week.

- In 1920 the government gave £500,000 to the Central Committee for Women's Training and Employment. This set up centres to train women in hairdressing and horticulture, journalism and domestic work. But by 1921, only training for domestic service was being financially supported.

Discrimination and disillusionment

Many women were severely criticised and even vilified for retaining jobs that, in popular opinion, should have been 'given back' to the men. There were other ways, too, of curtailing women's ambitions:

- By the end of the war, some 56 per cent of civil service employees were women. The 1919 civil service re-organisation replaced many experienced, well-qualified women by unqualified, inexperienced men. Women were segregated from men and set to work in lower grade positions. This resulted in men gaining ready promotion over better-qualified women.

- The government failed fully to implement the Sex Disqualification (Removal) Act, in particular by reserving particular posts in the civil service for men only.

- In a test case, it was ruled that a married woman could be barred from teaching because married women did not have the right to employment. Within months, London County Council had introduced a ban on all married teachers.

- By 1926, 75 per cent of local authorities had imposed similar restrictions on the employment of married women.

- Women doctors, nurses and health workers were dismissed when they got married.

- Domestic service continued to be the largest source of employment and, by 1931, 35 per cent of all working women were in domestic service.

- The textile industry, the second largest employer of women, facing a recession, successfully implemented wage cuts for female workers and instigated work practices favourable to men.

Focus on the positive

The government may have failed to implement the Sex Disqualification (Removal) Act insofar as the civil service was concerned, but the Act was implemented in respect of entry to the professions. Seventy-seven women had succeeded in becoming barristers by 1927. The numbers of women entering the medical profession had risen from 6 per cent in 1911 to 7.4 per cent in 1925, a miniscule rise, but a rise nonetheless. In general terms, the employment of women in shop-keeping and clerical work rose considerably, as did, but to a lesser extent, the numbers of women working in banking and accounting. The growth of light industries in the midlands

> **Question**
>
> By 1929 Britain was facing a serious economic depression. Can, therefore, these measures be seen as anti-women?

and south-east provided opportunities for women able to tolerate the tedium of chocolate-box filling and radio wiring. However, women continued to earn half that of men for doing the same work, the differentials in unemployment benefits continued, and women were inevitably channelled into routine, less skilled work. Finally, the marriage ban continued to deter women from pursuing careers, facing them with an unenviable choice and almost inevitably placing them under the economic control of their husbands.

Source V

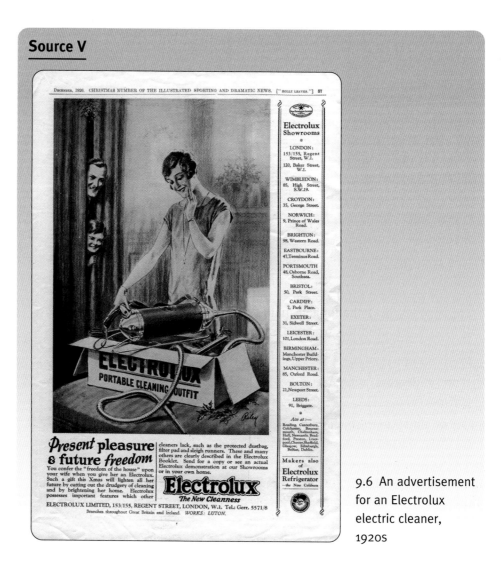

9.6 An advertisement for an Electrolux electric cleaner, 1920s

Question

How far had the 'separate spheres' and 'angel in the house' philosophies vanished by the 1920s?

Unit summary

What have you learned in this unit?

You have learned that in the years before the First World War, women had made significant advances in the world of work. Even though domestic work claimed most women workers, the textile industry expanded greatly because of the mill-girl workforce. The professions, too, were beginning to open their doors to women. Women were beginning to organise themselves within the trade union movement, sometimes with the help of male trade unionists. The First World War seemed initially to mark a turning point in women's employment. Single and married women were encouraged into the workplace, though not without misgivings on the part of government and trade unionists. By 1918, over 4 million women were at work and their efforts made an enormous contribution to eventual victory for the allies. The ending of the war in 1918 resulting in the return of over 3 million job-seeking demobbed men; the need to wind down the British economy to a peacetime level and the ensuing economic depression meant that millions of women lost their jobs. Those who remained in the workplace, or who joined it in the 1920s, found that their pay and conditions were very much worse than their male colleagues.

What skills have you used in this unit?

You have analysed a painting and tested the inferences you made from it against your own knowledge. You have worked with data to analyse change and continuity in women's work outside the home between the years 1851 and 1911. You have evaluated a number of sources relating to the most common occupation: domestic service, and have used this evaluation to help develop an understanding of why so many young women preferred to work in a factory and were attracted by shop work. You have worked with a number of sources and evaluating them has helped your understanding of why it was so difficult for women to enter the professions and of the ways in which young women (particularly those intending to follow a career in medicine) challenged male perceptions of the female role. You have considered the ways in which legislation might have helped women in the workplace, and understand that not all Acts were appreciated by all working women. You have cross-referenced a range of sources to begin to understand the somewhat complex attitude of trade unions to working women and vice versa. Your evaluation of sources, linked to your own knowledge, has helped you to understand the impact of the First World War on women's employment. Finally, you have used your knowledge and understanding of the source material to consider how far the concepts of the 'angel in the house' and 'separate spheres' had vanished by the 1920s.

And finally . . .

There is a story, which may or may not be true, that one day three girls sat chatting. Emily and Elizabeth were friends, and Millicent was Elizabeth's younger sister.

> 'Well', said Emily, 'it is clear enough what has to be done: you, Elizabeth, must open the medical profession to women. I must see to higher education. As the vote will follow the other two, Milly here, who is younger than we are, must attend to that.'

When they grew up, they did precisely that, didn't they?

SKILLS BUILDER

1 How far do you think the acceptance of middle-class women in the workplace was due to the need to solve the surplus women problem? Discuss this in your group. (You'll need to look back to page 6.)

2 Look at the ways in which women trade unionists operated. Do you think surveys and pressure groups (Source P) or direct action, as in the Match Girls' Strike, were the best way to get results?

3 In the 1920s, Britain was facing an economic crisis and depression. Was it right, in those circumstances, to dismiss the women from their jobs before the men?

Exam tips

This is the sort of question you will find appearing on the examination paper as a (b) question.

4 Study Sources T and U and use your own knowledge.

Do you agree with the view that women gained nothing from their wartime experiences?

You have worked on (b) style questions at the end of Units 2, 4, 6 and 7.

You have experimented with different sorts of plans and considered different styles of question.

You should now have a good idea of the way in which you prefer to plan your answer. So go ahead and plan an answer to this question.

Now test yourself! Look at your plan and check what you have drawn up. Have you:

- **Analysed** Sources T and U for points that **support** and points that **challenge** the view that women gained nothing from their wartime experiences, and noted these points in your plan?
- Shown how you will **cross-reference** between the sources for points of **agreement** and **disagreement**?
- Shown where you will use your **wider knowledge** both to **reinforce** and **challenge** the points you have derived from the sources?
- Thought about how you will **combine** the points you have made into an argument **for** or **against** the view that women gained nothing from their wartime experience, and noted this on your plan?
- Shown how your **evaluation** of the points you have used in argument has considered the **quality** of the **evidence** used?
- Noted what your **conclusion** will be, and how you will ensure it is **balanced** and **supported**?

RESEARCH TASK

- Who were the Ladies of Langham Place?
- What did they do to help open up the world of work for women?

OVERVIEW TASKS

Now that you have worked through the book, assemble evidence to answer these questions:

- To what extent had the 'angel in the house' and 'separate spheres' philosophies been shattered by 1930?
- What was the main agent of change affecting the position of women c.1860–1930?
- How far had women achieved equality with men by 1930?

Thematic review: source-based debate and evaluation

It is important, especially when dealing with a topic that addresses change over time, to stand back and review the period you have been studying. You need to ask yourself not only what happened, but why it happened and why it happened then and not, say, 100 years earlier or twenty years later. What had driven change? Which factors were significant and which were not? Were there any events that were critical turning points? Thematic review questions, spanning the whole time period, will help to focus your thinking. These are the thematic review questions that relate to 'The Changing Position of Women and the Suffrage Question c.1860–1930'. You can probably think of more, but for the moment these are the ones with which you will be working.

- How far did women achieve greater control over their personal lives in the period 1860–1930?

- To what extent had the ideologies of 'separate spheres' and 'angel in the house' been overturned by 1930?

- How significant to the changing role of women 1860–1930 was female enfranchisement?

- To what extent was education the key to change in women's roles during this period?

- How far had women's contribution to the world of work changed in the period 1860–1930?

Choose one of these thematic review questions that you plan to answer. Working through this section will make much more sense if you have an actual question in mind.

Answering a thematic review question

There are two key approaches to answering a thematic review question: **select** and **deploy**.

Select   You need to select appropriate source material. You need to select appropriate knowledge.

Deploy   You need to deploy what you have selected so that you answer the question in as direct a way as possible.

Unpacking 'select'

You will see that all the thematic review questions are asking for an evaluation. They ask 'How far . . .', 'To what extent . . .', 'How significant . . .', which means that you will have to weigh up the evidence given by the sources you have selected. You will, therefore, have to select sources that will give you a range of evidence. Six diary entries, for example, will not give you the range you want. You will also need to select sources that seem to provide evidence that pulls in different directions. Eight sources saying more or less the same thing but in different ways will not help you weigh up the significance of different sorts of evidence and reach a reasoned, supported conclusion.

So now go ahead.

(i) Look back through this book and select the sources, primary and secondary, that you think will give you the appropriate range, balance and evidence.

(ii) Make notes of the knowledge you will need to use to contextualise the   sources and create an argument.

You can't, of course, simply put some sources into an answer and hope that whoever is reading what you have written can sort things out for themselves. You need to evaluate the sources you have selected and use that evaluation to create the argument you will be making when you answer the question. You have already had practice of doing this, but here is a reminder of some of the questions you will need to ask of a source before you can turn it into evidence:

- Is the **content** appropriate for the question I am answering?

- Can I supply the appropriate **context** for the source?

- How **reliable** is the source as evidence? Was the author or artist **in a position to know** what he or she was talking about or painting?

- What was the intended **audience** of the source? What was the **purpose** of the source?

- If the source is a photograph, did the photographer **pose** the people in the picture? Was the photographer **selective** in what he or she chose to photograph?

- How **useful** is this source in developing an answer to the question? Remember that a source that is unreliable can still be useful.

Now you have your selection of source material, you need to think about it as a package. Does it do the job you want it to do? Does it supply you with enough evidence to argue your case, while at the same time providing you with enough evidence of different points of view so that you can show you have considered what weight the evidence will bear in reaching a reasoned, supported conclusion? In other words, can you effectively **cross-reference** between the sources, showing where they support and where they challenge each other?

Unpacking 'deploy'

The key to successful deployment of evidence and knowledge in answering a question like the one you have selected is always to keep the question in the forefront of your mind. Keep focused! Don't be tempted to go off into interesting by-ways. Make every paragraph count as you build your argument.

You have already had a lot of practice in essay planning and writing, so this is just a reminder of the main things you need to bear in mind.

Plan	Plan carefully how you are going to construct your answer and make out your case.
Structure	You should structure your answer (you can use this framework as a guide).
Introduction	'Set out your stall', briefly outlining your argument and approach.
Paragraphs	The main body of your answer should develop your argument, using the evidence you have gathered by questioning the sources. As you outline your case, remember to cross-reference between the sources that you are using, and to show on which source you place the greater weight.
Conclusion	This should demonstrate that you have weighed up the evidence in order to reach your conclusion. It will pull your case together, giving a supported summary of your arguments and show how you reached a reasoned judgement.

In other words, say what you are going to do, do it, and show that you have done it.

You do not, of course, have to respond to these thematic review questions by writing an essay all by yourself. You could work collaboratively in a small group, or you could use one or more of the questions to prepare for a class debate. In whatever way you are going to use these thematic review questions, the approach will be the same: select, deploy and keep to the point.

Good luck!

Exam zone

Hot tips

What other students have said

FROM GCSE TO AS LEVEL

'I really enjoyed studying modern world history at GCSE but I am glad that I had the chance to look at some nineteenth- and twentieth-century English history at AS level. It has been challenging but enjoyable to study a different period.'

'Many of the skills that I learned at GCSE were built upon at AS level, especially in Unit 2 where the skills of source evaluation and analysis are very important.'

'AS level history seems like a big step up at first with more demands made on independent reading and more complex source passages to cope with. However by the end of the first term I felt as if my written work had improved considerably.'

'The more practice source-based questions I attempted, the more confident I became and quite quickly I picked up the necessary style and technique required for success.'

'I found it really helpful to look at the mark schemes in the textbook. It was reassuring to see what the examiners were looking for and how I could gain top marks.'

WHAT I WISH I HAD KNOWN AT THE START OF THE YEAR

'I used the textbook a lot during the revision period to learn the key facts and practise key skills. I really wished that I had used it from the beginning of the course in order to consolidate my class notes.'

'I wished that I had taken more time reading and noting other material such as the photocopied handouts issued by my teacher. Reading around the subject and undertaking independent research would have made my understanding more complete and made the whole topic more interesting.'

'AS history is not just about learning the relevant material but also developing the skills to use it effectively. I wish that I had spent more time throughout the year practising source questions to improve my style and technique.'

'I wish I had paid more attention to the advice and comments made by my teacher on the written work I had done. This would have helped me to improve my scores throughout the year.'

HOW TO REVISE

'I started my revision by buying a new folder and some dividers. I put all my revision work into this folder and used the dividers to separate the different topics. I really took pride in my revision notes and made them as thorough and effective as I could manage.'

'Before I started the revision process, I found it helpful to plan out my history revision. I used the Edexcel specification given to me by my teacher as a guideline for which topics to revise and I ticked off each one as I covered it.'

'I found it useful to revise in short, sharp bursts. I would set myself a target of revising one particular topic in an hour and a half. I would spend one hour taking revision notes and then half an hour testing myself with a short practice question or a facts test.'

'I found it useful to always include some practice work in my revision. If I could get that work to my teacher to mark, then all the better, but just attempting questions to time helped me improve my technique.'

'Sometimes I found it helpful to revise with a friend. We might spend 45 minutes revising by ourselves and then half an hour testing each other. Often we were able to sort out any problems between us and it was reassuring to see that someone else had the same worries and pressures at that time.'

Refresh your memory

The following checklists provide the key points for each unit.

1 Mid-century women: philosophy and reality
   - The 'angel in the house'
   - The 'separate spheres' philosophy
   - The problem of unmarried and 'surplus' women
   - The extent to which reality mirrored and challenged the 'angel in the house' and 'separate spheres' philosophies.

2 How did women's personal lives change 1860–1901?
   - Double standards of sexual morality
   - The significance of Caroline Norton and the Jackson case in bringing about change
   - The importance of Josephine Butler and the campaign to repeal the Contagious Diseases Acts
   - Legislation allowing women greater control over their personal lives.

3 To what extent were women involved in public life before 1901?
   - Serving on school boards
   - Involvement in Poor Law administration
   - Activities in the Conservative and Liberal Parties
   - Working as municipal councillors.

4 Suffragists: getting started c.1860–c.1903
   - What were the arguments for and against giving women the vote?
   - The significance of the 1867 Reform Act
   - The importance of Lily Maxwell, Lydia Becker and Richard Pankhurst
   - The formation of the NUWSS.

5 Adding militancy to the campaign 1903–14
   - The reasons why the Pankhursts began their militant campaign
   - The structure of the WSPU and the attitudes of the organisation to working-class women
   - Support for the suffrage campaigns of the NUWSS and WSPU
   - The ways in which the militant campaigns changed in the years to 1914, including Black Friday and the death of Emily Davison.

6 The women's suffrage question: action and reaction
   - The attitudes of the Liberal government and the Conservative and Labour Parties to women's suffrage
   - Support given to women's suffrage by religious institutions, the media and trade unions.
   - The significance of the Conciliation Bills and the reasons for their failure
   - The ways in which the Liberal government dealt with suffragette militancy
   - The nature and impact of the anti-suffragist campaign.

7 1914 to 1928: a changed political landscape?
   - The ways in which the different suffrage societies reacted to the outbreak of war in 1914
   - Women's war work and impact on gaining the franchise
   - The significance of the Speaker's Conference of 1916
   - The reasons why women were enfranchised partially in 1918 and fully in 1928.

8 Educating women and girls: the key to success?

- The importance of Forster's Act (1870) and later legislation in providing education for working-class girls

- The importance of Frances Mary Buss, Dorothea Beale and the GPDST in providing education for the daughters of the middle class

- The differences in the education provided for working-class and middle-class girls

- The opening of higher education to young women

9 Opening up the world of work

- Change and continuity in women's work in the years before 1914

- The extent to which legislation helped working women

- The attitudes of trade unions to working women

- The impact of the First World War on women's work and its aftermath.

This revision checklist looks very knowledge-based. The examination, however, will test your source-based skills as well. So remember that when dealing with sources you must be able to:

- comprehend a source and break it down into key points

- interpret a source, drawing inferences and deductions from it rather than treating it as a source of information. This may involve considering the language and tone used as well.

- cross-reference points of evidence between sources to reinforce and challenge

- evaluate the evidence by assessing its quality and its reliability in terms of how much weight it will bear and how secure are the conclusions that can be drawn from it. This may include considering the provenance of the source.

- deal with the sources as a set to build a body of evidence.

Understanding assessment

You have spent a lot of time working on plans and constructing answers to the (a) and (b) questions. In Units 1, 3 and 8 you worked with (a) questions; in Units 2, 4, 6, 7 and 9 you worked with (b) questions. So you now have a pretty good idea about how to plan an answer and write a response to the questions of the examination paper. But what are the examiners looking for? And what marks will you get?

What will the exam paper look like?

There will be three questions on the paper.

(a) Compulsory: everyone has to do this.

(b) (i) and (b) (ii) You will have a choice here and will only have to answer one (b) question.

Sources There will be nine sources on the examination paper. But don't worry: you won't have to deal with them all! You'll only need to deal with six sources – three for each of the questions you will be answering. And here is the good news. So far, you have worked with very long sources, some of which were complicated. In the examination, because you will only have one hour and twenty minutes to answer the two questions, the sources will be much shorter. You'll probably be dealing with no more than around 550 words altogether.

Question (a) What will you have to do, and what marks will you get for doing it?

(a) You will have to focus on reaching a judgement by analysis, cross-referencing and evaluation of source material. The maximum number of marks you can get is 20. You will be working at any one of four levels. Try to get as high up in the levels as you can. Remember that the only knowledge, outside of that which you can find in the sources, is what examiners call 'contextual' knowledge. This means you can write enough to enable you to interpret the source, but no more. For example, if one of the three sources is by Emmeline Pankhurst, you should show the examiners that you know she is the leader of the WSPU, which is an organisation pressing for women's suffrage by militant means, but you should not describe the way in which the WSPU was organised, nor the militant acts members carried out unless this information helps the understanding of a particular source.

Level 1 Have you shown that you understand the surface features of the sources, and have you shown that you have selected material relevant to the question? Does your response consist mainly of direct quotations from the sources?

1–5 marks *This is what you will score.*

Level 2 Have you identified points of similarity and difference in the sources in relation to the question asked? Have you made at least one developed comparison or a range of undeveloped ones? Have you summarised the information you have found in the sources? Have you noted the provenance of at least one of the sources?

6–10 marks *This is what you will score.*

Level 3 Have you cross-referenced between the sources, making detailed comparisons supported by evidence from the sources? Have you shown that you understand you have to weigh the evidence by looking at the nature, origins, purpose and audience of the sources? Have you shown you have thought about considering 'how far' by trying to use the sources as a set?

11–15 marks *This is what you will score.*

Level 4 Have you reached a judgement in relation to the issue posed by the question? Is this judgement supported by careful examination of the evidence of the sources? Have you cross-referenced between the sources and analysed the points of similarity and disagreement? Have you taken account of the different qualities of the sources in order to establish what weight the evidence will bear? Have you used the sources as a set when addressing 'how far' in the question?

16–20 marks *This is what you will score.*

Now try this (a) question:

(a) Study Sources A, B and C. How far do Sources A and B challenge the views expressed in Source C?

Source A

Women's suffrage is dangerous because of the vast growth of the Empire, the immense increase of England's imperial responsibilities and the increased complexity of the problems which lie before our statesmen. These problems can only be solved by the labour and special knowledge of men, and where the men who bear the burden ought to be left unhampered by the political inexperience of women.

Part of a letter written by Mrs Humphrey Ward and published in The Times on 27 February 1909

Source B

Lady Musgrave, President of the East Grinstead branch of the Anti-Suffragette League said she was strongly against the franchise being extended to women, for she did not think it would do any good whatsoever. Women were not equal to men in endurance or nervous energy, and, she thought she might say, on the whole, in intellect. Women have not had the political experience that men have and, on the whole, did not want the vote, and had little knowledge of, or interest in, politics. Politics would go on without the help of women, but the home wouldn't.

Part of a report published in the East Grinstead Observer on 27 May 1911

Source C

This difference between men and women, instead of being a reason against their enfranchisement, seems to me the strongest possible reason in favour of it; we want the home and the domestic side of things to count for more in politics and in the administrations of public affairs than they do at present. We want to know how various kinds of legislative enactments bear on the home and domestic life.

From Millicent Fawcett in a pamphlet Home and Politics date of publication unknown

Now use the marking criteria to assess your response.

How did you do?

What could you have done to have achieved a better mark?

Question (b) What will you have to do and what marks will you get for doing it?

(b)   You will have to analyse and evaluate a historical view or claim using two sources and your own knowledge. There are 40 marks for this question. You will get 24 marks for your own knowledge and 16 marks for your source evaluation. You can be working at any one of four levels. Try to get as high up in the levels as you can. The examiners will be marking your answer twice: once for knowledge and a second time for source evaluation.

This is what the examiners will be looking for as they mark the ways in which you have selected and used your knowledge to answer the question:

Level 1   Have you written in simple sentences without making any links between them? Have you provided only limited support for the points you are making? Have you written what you know separately from the sources? Is what you have written mostly generalised and not really directed at the focus of the question? Have you made a lot of spelling mistakes and is your answer disorganised?

1–6 marks   *This is what you will score.*

Level 2   Have you produced a series of statements that are supported by mostly accurate and relevant factual material? Have you made some limited links between the statements you have written? Is your answer mainly 'telling the story' and not really analysing what happened? Have you kept your own knowledge and the sources separate? Have you made a judgement that isn't supported by facts? Is your answer a bit disorganised with some spelling and grammatical mistakes?

7–12 marks   *This is what you will score.*

Level 3   Is your answer focused on the question? Have you shown that you understand the key issues involved? Have you included a lot of descriptive material along with your analysis of the issues? Is your material factually accurate but a bit lacking in depth and/or relevance? Have you begun to integrate your own knowledge with the source material? Have you made a few spelling and grammatical mistakes? Is your work mostly well organised?

13–18 marks *This is what you will score.*

Level 4   Does your answer relate well to the question focus? Have you shown that you understand the issues involved? Have you analysed the key issues? Is the material you have used relevant to the question and factually accurate? Have you begun to integrate what you know with the evidence you have gleaned from the source material? Is the material you have selected balanced? Is the way you have expressed your answer clear and coherent? Is your spelling and grammar mostly accurate?

19–24 marks *This is what you will score.*

This is what the examiners are looking for as they mark your source evaluation skills.

Level 1	Have you shown that you understand the sources? Is the material you have selected from them relevant to the question? Is your answer mostly direct quotations from the sources or re-writes of them in your own words?
1–4 marks	*This is what you will score.*
Level 2	Have you shown that you understand the sources? Have you selected from them in order to support or challenge from the view given in the question? Have you used the sources mainly as sources of information?
5–8 marks	*This is what you will score.*
Level 3	Have you analysed the sources, drawing from them points of challenge and/or support for the view contained in the question? Have you developed these points, using the source material? Have you shown that you realise you are dealing with just one viewpoint and that the sources point to other, perhaps equally valid ones? Have you reached a judgement? Have you supported that judgement with evidence from the sources?
9–12 marks	*This is what you will score.*
Level 4	Have you analysed the sources, raising issues from them? Have you discussed the viewpoint in the question by relating it to the issues raised by your analysis of the source material? Have you weighed the evidence in order to reach a judgement? Is your judgement fully explained and supported by carefully selected evidence?
13–16 marks	*This is what you will score.*

Now try this (b) question:

(b) Read Sources D, E and F and use your own knowledge.

Do you agree with the view, expressed in Source F, that involvement in local government inhibited, rather than helped, women's progress towards being allowed to vote in parliamentary elections?

Source D

The Committee on School Accommodation and Attendance has to enforce the by-laws dealing with attendance at school of all the children, including the blind, deaf, difficult and crippled children; it watches the growth and shifting of population, and decides on the districts in which additional school provision is needed, and decides where a new site should be acquired or an old one disposed of; it also watches all bills in parliament which affect the Board's work, and conducts most of the Board's correspondence with the Education Department.

Miss Davenport Hill and Mrs Homan were on this committee.

From *Women on School Boards* written by Florence Davenport Hill in 1896. Florence was a social reformer and strong supporter of women's suffrage. Here she is writing about the work of the London school board committees.

Source E

The most impressive feature of this great meeting was the presence of hundreds of women who were a component part, a vital factor, in what today is one of the greatest political organisations in England. There were women officers and delegates, equal in authority with men. Fully a third of them – every woman householder – was entitled to vote at all except the parliamentary elections, and they constituted what Liberal and Conservatives alike recognised and, what is more, respected – an active political influence which both parties were forced to accept as such.

> An American, Mary H. Krout, was a guest in 1896 at the annual Habitation of the Primrose League. This was a very grand affair, held in the Covent Garden Opera House. Lord Salisbury was the guest speaker and all the local Primrose League habitations sent delegates. Mary wrote about her experiences as a visitor to London in *A Looker-on in London* published in 1899. This is part of what she said about the 1896 annual Habitation.

Source F

Women believed that local government work would win them the vote. However, Liberals feared that propertied women would vote Tory; Tories, that female suffrage would challenge male authority. Gladstone had added that if married women got the vote, husbands would either have two votes or engage in marital dispute; yet if votes were confined to spinsters and widows, they would be rewarding those without a husband, the failures of their sex. So clearly you couldn't enfranchise any women. The Lords thought this argument very fetching.

Indeed, far from local government being a stepping-stone to the vote, it blocked it. Men now decided that there were two spheres of politics: the domestic – education, poor law, hospital work, which women could and should do; and imperial – war, commerce, empire, finance, which women clearly could not. Precisely because women found their appropriate service in local government, they were not needed, or wanted, at Westminster.

> From a speech made by Baroness Patricia Hollis to the AGM of the Women's Local Government Society in Sheffield Town Hall on 10 March 2007

Now use the marking criteria to assess your response.

How did you do?

What could you have done to have achieved higher marks?

The examiners will not be nit-picking their way through your answer, ticking things off as they go. Rather, they will be looking to see which levels best fit the response you have written to the question, and you should do the same when assessing your own responses.

How will I time my responses?

You have 1 hour 20 minutes to answer two questions. Remember that the (a) question is compulsory and that you will have a choice of one from two (b) questions. Take time, say, five minutes, to read through the paper and think about your choice of (b) question. The (a) question is worth half the marks of the (b) question, so you should aim to spend twice the time on the (b) question. This means that, including planning time, you should spend about 25 minutes on the (a) question and about 50 minutes (again, including planning) on the (b) question.

Practice questions

The following is a list of exam-style questions from each of the units in this book. The source references refer to the source references in each unit.

1 Mid-century women: philosophy and reality
   (i) Study Sources C, E and G.
   To what extent does Source G challenge the 'angel in the house' described in Sources C and E?
   (ii) Study Source H, J and K and use your own knowledge.
   How far do you agree with the view that Victorian society was divided into 'separate spheres'?

2 How did women's personal lives change 1860–1901?
   (i) How far do Sources G and H agree with Source J about the problems of prostitution?
   (ii) Study Sources L, M and N.
   To what extent do you agree that the campaign methods themselves were more important than the success of the campaign to repeal the Contagious Diseases Acts?

3 To what extent were women involved in public life before 1901?
   (i) Study Sources A, B and C.
   How far would you agree with the view that the concept of the 'angel in the house' was still underpinning attitudes to women's contribution to society towards the end of the nineteenth century?
   (ii) Read Sources D, K and M.
   How far would you agree with the view, expressed in Source M, that involvement in local government inhibited, rather than helped, women's progress towards the vote?

4 Suffragists: getting started c.1860–c.1903
   (i) Read Sources C, D and I.
   To what extent do the views expressed in Source I about female franchise challenge those expressed in Sources C and D?
   (ii) Read Sources I, M and N and use your own knowledge.
   How far do you agree with the view that suffrage reform would come if it was pursued in constitutional, legal ways?
   Read Sources F, G and H.
   How far does Source H challenge the effectiveness of women's work in administering the Poor Law described in Sources F and G?

5 Adding militancy to the campaign 1903–14
   (i) Read Sources C, D and I.
   To what extent do the views expressed in Source I about female franchise challenge those expressed in Sources C and D?
   (ii) Read Sources F, I and J and use your own knowledge.
   How far do you agree with the view, expressed in Source J, that there were surprising similarities between the arguments of those who supported, and those who opposed women's suffrage?

6 The women's suffrage question: action and reaction
   (i) Study Sources F, G and H.
   How far does Source H challenge the evidence of Sources F and G?
   (ii) Study Sources J, N and O and use your own knowledge.
   Do you agree with the view that the Liberal government was hostile to giving women the vote?

7 1918 to 1928: a changed political landscape?
   (i) Study Sources B C and D.
   How far do Sources C and D support what Emmeline Pankhurst is saying in Source B?
   (ii) Study Sources T and W and use your own knowledge.
   Do you agree with the view that political expediency was the main factor in giving all women, in 1928, the vote on the same terms as men?

8 Educating women and girls: the key to success?
   (i) Study Sources H and I and use your own knowledge.
   Do you agree with the view, expressed in Source I, that 'schooling secured woman's imprisonment in domesticity'?
   (ii) Study Sources L and R and use your own knowledge
   Do you agree with the view that schools such as the North London Collegiate School and Cheltenham Ladies' College perpetuated class divisions among girls and their families?

9 Opening up the world of work
   i) Study Sources E, F and G.
   How far does Source E challenge the views expressed in Sources F and G?
   (ii) Study Sources R and S and use your own knowledge.
   Do you agree with the view, expressed in Source S, that the changes affecting women 1914–18 were very dependent upon changes affecting men?

You have now had a lot of practice in planning, writing and assessing your responses to the sort of questions you can expect to find on the examination paper. You are well prepared and you should be able to tackle the examination with confidence. *Good luck!*

References

Bartley, P. (1998) *Votes for Women 1860–1928*, Hodder & Stoughton Educational

Beale, D. (1871) *On the Education of Women*, publisher unknown

Beeton, I. (1861) *Beeton's Book of Household Management*, S.O. Beeton

Billington, R. (1985) 'Women, Politics and Local Liberalism: From "Female Suffrage" to "Votes for Women"', *Journal for Regional and Local Studies*, vol. 5

Billington-Grieg, T. (1907) *Women's Liberty and Men's Fear*, publisher unknown

Blackstone, W. (1765) *Commentaries on the Laws of England*, Clarendon Press

Booth, C. (1886) *Journal of the Royal Historical Society*, Royal Historical Society

Brooks, D.C. (1970) *The Emancipation of Women*, Macmillan

Butler, J. (1896) *Personal Reminiscences of a Great Crusade*, H. Marshall & Son

Davenport Hill, F. (1896) *Women on School Boards*, publisher unknown

Davin, A. (1978) 'A Centre of Humanising Influence': The Schooling of Working-class Girls Under the London School Board 1870–1902*, unpublished paper

D'Cruze, S. (1995) *Women and the Family*, publisher unknown

Dyhouse, C. (1987) 'Miss Buss and Miss Beale: Gender and Authority in the Field of Education', in F. Hunt (ed.) *Lessons for Life*, Basil Blackwell

Fisher, T. (1996) 'Josephine Butler: Feminism's Neglected Pioneer', *History Today*, Vol. 46(6), June

The General Baptist Repository and Missionary Observer, 1840

Graveson, R.H. (1957) *A Century of Family Law 1857–1957*, Sweet & Maxwell

Harrison, B. (1978) *Separate Spheres: The Opposition to Women's Suffrage in Britain*, Croom Helm

Harrison, B. (1983) 'Women's Suffrage at Westminster 1866–1928', in M. Bentley and J. Stevenson (eds.) *High and Low Politics in Modern Britain: Ten Studies*, Oxford University Press

Hirshfield, C. (1990) 'Fractured Faith: Liberal Party Women and the Suffrage Issue in Britain 1892–1914', *Gender and History*, Vol. 2(2)

Hubback, E. (1928) 'The Equal Franchise', *Fortnightly Review*, April

Hubbard, L. (1878) *Duties of Women as School Managers*, publisher unknown

Hunt, F. (ed.) (1987) *Lessons for Life: The Schooling of Girls and Women 1850–1950*, Basil Blackwell

Jarrold & Sons (1871) *New Code Reading Books II*, Jarrold & Sons

John, A.V. (ed.) (1985) *Unequal Opportunities: Women's Employment in England 1800–1918*, Basil Blackwell

Krout, M. H. (1899) *A Looker-on in London*, Dodd, Mead and Company

The Lancet, August 1912

Manton, J. (1965) *Elizabeth Garrett Anderson*, Methuen

Martindale, H. (1944) *From One Generation to Another 1839–1944*, George Allen & Unwin Ltd

Marwick, A. (1965) *The Deluge: British Society and the First World War*, Bodley Head

Marwick, A. (1977) *Women at War 1914–1918*, Croom Helm

Mayer, A. (2002) *Women in Britain 1900–2000*, Hodder & Stoughton

J.D. Milne (1857) *The Industrial and Social Position of Women*, publisher unknown

Mitchell, H. (1977) *The Hard Way Up: Autobiography*, Virago

National Review, April 1862

Nightingale, F. (written in 1854) *Cassandra*, published as an appendix to R. Strachey (1928) *The Cause: A Short History of the Women's Movement in Great Britain*, G. Bell and Sons Ltd

The Nineteenth Century, August 1890

Norton, C. (1854) *English Laws for Women in the Nineteenth Century*, published privately

Central Society for Women's Suffrage (1905) *Opinions of Leaders of Religious Thought*, Central Society for Women's Suffrage

Pankhurst, C. (1959) *Unshackled: The Story of How We Won the Vote*, Hutchinson

Pankhurst, E. (1914) *My Own Story*, Nash

Pankhurst, S. (1931) *The Suffrage Movement: An Intimate Account of Persons and Ideals*, Longmans

Paterson, E. (1879) *The Women's Union Journal*, Women's Trade Union League

Patmore, C. (1854) *The Angel in the House*, John W. Parker and Son

Phillips, M. (2003) *The Ascent of Women*, Little, Brown

Pugh, M. (1985) *The Tories and the People 1880–1935*, B. Blackwell

Pugh, M. (1994) *Votes for Women in Britain 1867–1928*, The Historical Association

Pugh, M. (2000) *The March of the Women: A Revisionist Analysis of the Campaign for Women's Suffrage, 1866–1914*, Oxford University Press

Purvis, J. (2000) 'Emmeline Pankhurst (1858–1928) and Votes for Women', in J. Purvis and S. Holton *Votes for Women*, Routledge

Quarterly Review (1867) Vol. 123, John Murray

Raikes, E. (1908) *Dorothea Beale of Cheltenham*, Archibald Constable

Rees, R. (1986) *Social and Political Change in England: Margaret McMillan and the Battle for the Slum Child*, Longman Resources Unit

Ruskin, J. (1865) *Sesame and Lilies*, John Wiley & Son

Sanderson, M. (1983) *Education, Economic Change and Society in England 1780–1870*, Macmillan

Sewell, S. (1868) *Women and the Times We Live In*, publisher unknown

Smith, H.L. (1998) *The British Women's Suffrage Campaign 1866–1928*, Longman

Strachey, R. (1928) *The Cause: A Short History of the Women's Movement in Great Britain*, G. Bell and Sons Ltd

The Suffragette (1912) 'Emmeline Pankhurst at the Albert Hall', 25 October

Taine, H. (1885) *Notes on England*, Chapman & Hall

Tennyson, Lord A. (1847) *The Princess*, E. Moxon

Turnbull, A. (1987) 'Learning Her Womanly Work: The Elementary School Curriculum 1870–1914', in F. Hunt (ed.) *Lessons for Life: The Schooling of Girls And Women 1850–1950*, Basil Blackwell

Women's Union Journal, 1877

WSPU *Annual Report*, 1914

Glossary

Amendment An amendment to a parliamentary bill is a change that an MP, or group of MPs, would like to make to the bill. Then, as now, MPs vote on the amendments before they vote on the actual bill.

'Angel in the house' In 1854 Coventry Patmore wrote a poem called 'The Angel in the House'. In the poem, he made it clear that a wife's function was to please her husband, not just in his bed but by making his home a peaceful haven from the troubles and strains of the world, and by bringing up his children properly. She was, in fact, the 'angel in the house', bringing peace, love and contentment to all and never considering her own wants and needs.

Annuities A yearly allowance: a sum of money paid to an individual every year.

Annulment When a marriage is annulled it is as if, legally, it never happened. An annulment is usually granted when sexual intercourse has not occurred. An annulment is different from a divorce, when sexual intercourse has happened and there are often children as a result.

Case law English law is based on case law. The way in which a particular judge interprets a law will be used by future judges when they have to make their decisions. All these decisions, taken together, form case law.

Conscientious objectors People whose consciences would not let them fight.

Dame schools Small private schools that provided an education for working-class children before they were old enough to work. Usually run by elderly women, dame schools charged around 3d a week to teach children to read and write. Some were good; others were little more than child-minders.

Denominational Connected to one of the branches of the Christian church.

Domestic service This phrase usually relates to the work women do in rich and well-to-do homes. They work as cooks and kitchen maids, as ladies' maids and nursery maids, as housemaids and housekeepers. Men also enter domestic service, but as butlers, valets and boot-boys.

Enumerator Literally, an enumerator is a person who counts. In this context, an enumerator was the person who took the census. Enumerators visited every house on census night and listed everyone who was living there with, after 1851, details of where they were born and what work they did.

Female emancipation To emancipate a person or a specific group of people (such as slaves) literally means to release them from control or restraint. In this context, therefore, female emancipation means to release women from legislative and social controls that prevented them from participating in society on the same terms as men.

Franchise The right to vote in public elections.

The Irish Question In the nineteenth and twentieth centuries, the 'Irish Question' focused on whether to give Home Rule to the whole island of Ireland, or to divide the island into Ulster and Eire or to continue to rule the whole island from Westminster.

'Leap in the dark' A phrase used about the 1867 Reform Bill, because no one was sure what impact giving the vote to 700,000 skilled workers would have on the House of Commons.

Legal identity To be recognised by the law. In the case of married women at this time, they were not recognised as being legally separate people from their husbands.

Lord Chancellor Person responsible for government policy on the legal system, head of the judiciary and presides over the House of Lords.

Militant Aggressively active in pursuing a social or political end. Militancy means being involved in militant activities.

Narrative painting A painting that tells a story.

Non-denominational Not connected to any particular religious group.

Non-partisan Not committed to any side.

Non-sectarian education An education not based on religion or religious principles.

Pariah A social outcast.

Parliamentary divisions Members of parliament register their votes on specific bills, debates and in committees by dividing. The results of the vote are referred to as Divisions. The Division List records how MPs have voted. The same process happens in the House of Lords.

Parliamentary whips Whips are the MPs who are appointed by party leaders to manage, and if necessary, discipline, MPs in their own political party. They can, for example, insist that party members vote in a particular way.

People's Budget A budget introduced in 1909 by the Chancellor of the Exchequer, David Lloyd George. In it he funded both old age pensions (an entirely new idea) and a Dreadnought battleship building programme by imposing new taxes on the rich. This enraged the Conservative Party (who had a majority in the House of Lords) and precipitated a constitutional crisis when the Lords rejected the budget.

Poor Law guardian All workhouses had guardians. These were people elected by the local community to make sure they were run properly.

Private Members' Bills A bill drawn up and proposed by an individual member of parliament without any government involvement.

Separate spheres This is the idea that men and women occupy separate and different spheres in society. Men work outside the home, in factories, offices and in government. Women work inside the home, making sure it is a fitting refuge for men from the stresses and strains of everyday life.

Suffrage The right to vote.

Sweated industries Instead of giving a job to a craftsman, it would be handed over to a middleman or woman, known as a 'sweater'. He or she would take it round to the home of an unskilled worker, usually a woman, who would do the work for very low pay. Often this work was broken down into a series of small jobs, each attracting a very small amount of money.

TB (Tuberculosis) A deadly and infectious disease commonly affecting the lungs. Such was the serious and widespread nature of the disease it is estimated to have been responsible for one third of all deaths in the early nineteenth century.

Trust In the sense that the word is used here, it is a legal term referring to the way in which an organisation is set up and run. In this case, a group of people, called trustees, were set up to run a number of schools. This ensured that all schools in the Trust had the same aims and worked to the same principles.

Universal manhood suffrage Giving the vote to all adult men.

Veto powers of the House of Lords One outcome of the constitutional crisis precipitated by the House of Lords' rejection of the People's Budget (see page 86) was the Parliament Act of 1911. By this Act the House of Lords could no longer veto bills: it could only delay them.

Women's Land Army The Women's Land Army was established by the government in order to persuade women to work in agriculture. This was necessary because of the large numbers of farm labourers who had enlisted in the armed forces, and because of the need for Britain to become more self-sufficient in terms of foodstuffs. By 1917 there were over 260,000 women working as farm labourers.

Index

Page references in *italics* indicate illustrations.